AN
EVANGELICAL
THEOLOGY OF
PREACHING

DONALD ENGLISH

ABINGDON PRESS
Nashville

AN EVANGELICAL THEOLOGY OF PREACHING

Copyright © 1996 by Abingdon Press

Library of Congress Cataloging-in-Publication Data

English, Donald.
    An evangelical theology of preaching / Donald English.
        p.   cm.
    Includes bibliographical references.
    ISBN 0-687-12178-7 (pbk. : alk. paper)
    1. Preaching.   2. Evangelicalism.   I. Title.
    BV4211.2.E54   1996
    251—dc20   95-50581
                                                              CIP

Scripture quotations unless otherwise labeled are from the New Revised Standard Version Bible, Copyright © 1989 by the Division of Christian Education of the National Council of the Churches of Christ in the USA. Used by permission.

96 97 98 99 00 01 02 03 04 05—10 9 8 7 6 5 4 3 2 1

MANUFACTURED IN THE UNITED STATES OF AMERICA

Joe and Mary Hale
whose lives encourage preachers
all over the world

Contents

Foreword

In one sense, *An Evangelical Theology of Preaching* is written for the working pastor who may need a clarified vision of what the preaching vocation can be, and can achieve, in this generation. Pastors with such a need (and that is a majority of us) will find Donald English's book at least as helpful as any written in the 1990s. The author focuses primarily on *why* we communicate the gospel, and he helps us clarity *what* should be communicated to both God's people and the wider public in our secular age. He also devotes an exceedingly helpful chapter on the faithful (and interesting) interpretation of the different types of biblical texts and passages, and another on the identity, soul, and life of the person who preaches.

However, the population who needs this book is so much wider than preaching pastors that I have almost concluded that the book was tragically titled. At the least, the book deserves reading by anyone—Sunday school teachers, small group leaders, counselors, lay witnesses, and even Christian parents—who accept the privilege of interpreting or explaining the faith to other people. Indeed, the book warrants reading by all Christians who are trying to make fuller sense of their faith while living in a world that marginalizes the church. The author defines the task of "preaching" as "interpreting the Scripture in ways that [make] sense to the hearer." By that definition, all Christians have a stake in becoming effective "preachers."

The book's greatest contribution is its focus upon the mission of Christian theology in a secular world that will not sit still and be a fixed target for the reflecting church, a world that presents a parade of challenges—from the traditional challenges like faith vis-à-vis reason and science, to newer challenges like moral and ethical relativism, genetics, and the Internet. Dr. English believes that "evangelical" theology provides the framework for addressing this changing world, and its peoples, most faithfully and effectively.

Most readers will not find Donald English's theology to be "evangelical" in a narrow or dogmatic sense—although Christians stuck in Enlightenment relativism and unreconstructed liberalism, still believing that all religions are more or less "the same," will find the book disconfirming. The writer draws from the evangelical faith, Catholic and Protestant, that most thinking Christian have believed deeply in most of the eras of the Christian movement.

English is not uncritical of our doctrinal legacy. Indeed, he begins chapter three by suggesting: "The trouble with Christian doctrine is that it comes to us in creedal statements." Furthermore, by sketching out a new theory of the Atonement (while also affirming the several traditional theories), he models a way to stand on the shoulders of our forebearers and sometimes see farther.

Mainly, Donald English is an advocate of classical Christianity. He believes that people can be in living touch with the God who "is different from us but not distant from us," who is present in the midst of life to redeem. He believes that doctrine is "not intended to be a dead deposit from the past"; it is intended to inform our lives, including our public lives.

Indeed, Donald English believes that as Christians get in touch with the *meaning* of great biblical texts, and the *meaning* of doctrines like Creation, Incarnation, Redemption, Trinity, Holy Spirit, and Judgment, these will provide the most fruitful foundations for engaging pre-Christian people and the several sectors of secular society.

Many Christians (including preachers) who read this book very thoroughly will become convinced that Donald English can do what he is writing about. Much more important, they will become convinced that *they* can do what he is writing about! More than any other recent book I know, this book can help people move from spectators and consumers of the gospel to interpreters and advocates.

I was present in the large audience at Asbury Theological Seminary when Dr. English delivered several of these chapters in the inaugural series of our Beeson Lectureship on Preaching. We were aware at the time that we were privileged to be in on the beginning of an important project for the future church. I am now privileged to commend the whole project to a much wider audience.

George Hunter
Dean, E. Stanley Jones School of
World Mission and Evangelism,
Asbury Theological Seminary

Introduction

This is not another "method" book on preaching. There are many excellent books of that kind. This is rather a book about why anyone would want to preach in the first place. If it had a text it would be Peter's outburst in front of the religious authorities in Jerusalem. "We cannot keep from speaking about what we have seen and heard." *It is the message that both necessitates and inspires the preaching.*

There is a strong connection between the content of the message and the way in which it is preached, however. The gospel itself determines the need to preach, the content of the preaching, and the values by which preaching should be tested. So this is a book about why and what, with implications for how.

I first came across preaching in the mining villages and towns of the northeast of England where I grew up. I now realize that we had some good preachers among the ordained ministers. I recall clearly their varied preaching styles, and I learned a lot from them about what it means to be a Christian.

But it was the lay preachers—local preachers as they are described in British Methodism—who made a stronger impression on my memory and on my life as a Christian. I am still working out why that was so.

It was certainly the fact that they were local, and had mostly lived in their town or village for most or all of their lives. The history of the area was their history, and their roots went deeply into that soil. Their experience of life was shaped by that context (though some had been away for one of the two world wars). A fair proportion had responsibilities of a voluntary kind outside the church, all for the good of a rather run-down part of the nation. As they led worship and preached it was evident that they belonged in that area. John Wesley's holding together of evangelism, social concern, and political influence was natural to most of them. It was all part of being a Christian citizen.

There was also a sense in which their role as preacher was the most distinctive thing about them in the community. Many of them had what would be considered ordinary jobs in the hierarchy of business and industry. Not many were in management. A few were teachers, or became so after the Second World War. But in the main their daily work was not distinguished. It was their commitment to preaching that set them apart as different. Preaching was not so much what they did as what they were. I felt I would know most of them better along that avenue than along any other.

There was a third quality about these people. Since most had not had an extensive education, they seemed to me to work even harder at redeeming lost time once they had a vocation (to preach) that gave them an incentive to study. I was amazed at the weighty theological volumes some of them attempted, and at their developed capacity for discussing the implications of what they read.

Last, they had no doubt that the basis of their preaching was biblical. Wrestling with the text was what preaching was about. I do not believe that it would have seemed proper to them to begin a sermon without announcing a text. Their views of the Bible and of its authority were by no means monochrome. Discussion on that subject could be heated! But they did not doubt that the preacher's task was to expound the Scripture in ways that made sense to the hearer.

I mention these matters at this point because they were formative to my understanding. As I have grown as a Christian,

I have learned increasingly to treasure that beginning. I am glad to have this chance to pay tribute to those preachers, like Joseph Birch who first took me out preaching with him, who demonstrated to me the seriousness, the importance, and the great privilege of being a preacher.

The immediate cause of my moving toward writing about preaching was the invitation to give the first of the Beeson Lectures at Asbury Theological Seminary in Wilmore, Kentucky. The then president, Dr. David McKenna, and his wife, Janet, made gracious provision for the accommodation of my wife and me, while the faculty and student body welcomed us most warmly. I am glad to express my gratitude to them, and to offer good wishes to the present president of the seminary, Dr. Maxie Dunnam, and his wife, Jerry.

I am most grateful to Jan Dale her immense patience and skill in turning my handwriting and dictation into presentable text

My greatest fear in writing a book on preaching is that readers might gain the impression that there is some hidden set of principles which, once discovered and applied, somehow makes one an acceptable preacher. My hope is rather that what follows will inspire preachers and would-be preachers with the excitement of the message, and a vision of the very many ways in which the good news can be proclaimed, and of their own particular place in that range of possibilities. There is ecstasy and agony in preaching, but I doubt that there is a greater calling anywhere.

—1—
God Is Here
How Could You Tell?

A basic assumption running throughout the Bible is the idea that God is among God's people. In the beginning God "walks in the garden at the time of the evening breeze" (Gen. 3:8). As the people of Israel make their journey across the wilderness, they are led by "the cloud . . . by day, and fire . . . by night" (Exod. 40:38). Even when they do not wish for God's presence, they hear the divine voice through the prophets, "Thus says the LORD" (Amos 1:3, 6, 9, 11). In the New Testament, God is present in Jesus (John 14:8-14), and after Pentecost through the Holy Spirit given to every believer (Acts 2:1-4; Rom. 8:9). God's people without God's presence is a contradiction in terms!

This assumption is also central to worship. We sing our hymns to offer God praise and thanks for the whole of life. We say our prayers as a way of affirming that we depend on God at every moment. Our readings from the Scripture declare our obedience to the revealed will of God every moment of every day. Our offerings make plain once more that everything we have comes from and belongs to God. So we sing the words of Fred Pratt Green: "God is here! As we your people meet to offer praise and prayer. . . ." *HP 653*

Without this awareness much of our worship loses its life and meaning. Hymns become merely artistic activity; prayers are moments of human reflection; the readings an intellectual engagement; and the offering is a way of sustaining the economy of the church as a human institution. When

I asked the saintly Richard Wurmbrand, after his many years of imprisonment for his faith, how he found worship in British churches, he replied, "I miss the presence of the angels." The sense of the divine presence transforms a corporate performance into an act of worship, as nothing else can.

This awareness that God is present in worship is more than a basis for our preaching. It is fundamental to its content. Many, who in worship are happy to sing about God's presence, need a great deal of help about what it means. If we cannot comprehend it in worship, how are we to do so beyond the walls of the church and outside worship? The preacher dare not avoid so basic a reality.

The traditional theological way of addressing this issue has been to speak of God's immanence and transcendence; immanence meaning presence, transcendence often seeming therefore to mean distance. The difficulty of that way of thinking is that it creates a division within God's very being. What is more, it makes God subservient to spatial concepts in an unworthy way.

A former archbishop of Canterbury, Michael Ramsey, points us in the right direction. He makes it plain that transcendence is not about *distance* but about *difference.*

> God is near but God is different. God is here, but man is dependent. God's otherness is the otherness of the Creator to the creature; of the Saviour to the sinner; and it is for the creature still to worship the Creator and for the sinner still to ask for the Saviour's grace.[1]

To say that God is transcendent is not to distance God from the world. "Our Father in heaven" (Matt. 6:9) is not a reference to God's postal address! The God who is transcendent is different from us, but not distant from us. Preaching ought to make that clear.

David Jenkins offers a helpful way of stating the relationship between God's immanence and transcendence. He writes of "transcendence in the midst."[2] If Ramsey is affirming God's presence but preserving God's difference, Jenkins begins with God's difference, but wishes to stress the reality of God's presence.

The Bible is full of examples of transcendence in the midst. The call of Abraham, Moses' experience of the burning bush, Gideon's summons in the fields, Isaiah's vision in the temple, and the word of God to Amos tending his sheep are all such instances in the Old Testament (Genesis 12; Exodus 3; Judges 6; Isaiah 6; Amos 1). In the New Testament, the disciples are called as they do their work of fishing, Matthew as he collects taxes, and the woman at the well as she goes for water (Mark 1:16-20; Matt. 9: 9-13; John 4: 1-26). Again and again, people sense the presence of God and respond to the call that comes through the transcendent in the midst.

The question for the preacher is whether people can have such experiences today. Since we who stand in pulpits are facing those who live in the modern world, we cannot simply commend experiences from the past if they have no relevance in the present. From the worlds of theology and sociology come strong affirmations of the continuing experience of the transcendent in modern life.

Ian Ramsey wrote about what he called "disclosure situations"; those moments and experiences that defy natural explanation, needing something more to do them justice.[3] We may think of those experiences so deep as to seem timeless; so beautiful as to defy description; so inward that words don't begin to express their true nature; so profound that one feels only the "soul" could respond to them. It may be a piece of music, a natural scene, a lovely relationship, a beautiful action. It can also be a profound loss, a moment of aloneness, a sense of being gripped by mystery, a feeling of deep need. In those moments something is disclosed far deeper than any of our logical or natural explanations can account for. We feel we would be gullible to accept such explanations. Something—more precisely Someone—is being disclosed to us, if we can

—————17

but perceive what is happening. We touch the very center of the universe and its meaning. We may pass the experience by and try to forget, or we may ask what kind of a universe we inhabit where such things are experienced.

A similar perspective, this time from a professional sociologist, is offered by Peter Berger. His research asked whether modern men and women who had undergone an education based on enlightenment principles and dominated by the scientific and technological revolutions, showed any need for awareness of realities beyond the scope of such disciplines. His conclusion is that, in an age of "the alleged demise of the supernatural" he discovered that, "for whatever reasons, sizeable numbers of the species modern man have not lost the propensity for awe, for the uncanny, for all the possibilities that are legislated against by the canons of secularised rationality." [4]

Berger selects such evidence as our sense of justice. Why, after centuries of injustice, do I get so angry at injustice? Why not accept it as the norm? Or what about our incurable sense of hope? Why do we assure the crying child in the middle of the night that, "It will be all right, dear"? What rational evidence supports that general approach to life? Or is some deeper conviction at work? Where do we get the remarkable sense of humor that seems to flourish in the most dangerous situations? How do we find time to play games? Is life not so serious that we should spend all our time working to keep it right? Berger suggests that our humor and our games are ways in which we affirm, subconsciously, that life is serious, but that its demands are not ultimate. There is a more ultimate demand on us than even the most serious of life's requirements.

If these assertions are true then the role of the preacher becomes a much larger one than the textbooks often suggest. There is no conflict with the encouragement to study the Bible. That remains basic. Neither is there any lessening of the responsibility for reading of theology and other disciplines. That is the source of many of the insights set out above. But neither of these in itself, nor all of them together, produces a preacher.

The significant requirement at this point is that of *the preacher as observer*. We are required to have more than a grasp of the biblical and theological basis for affirming God's presence in the world—transcendence in the midst. We are expected to *recognize that presence when we see it*. It is said that 90 percent of the secret of being an artist lies in what you see; committing it to canvas is the minor part. Paul Cézanne wrote of Claude Monet, "He was only an eye, but my God what an eye!"[5] The cost of that approach is clear in the works of Monet. He doesn't simply paint haystacks. He paints (the same) haystacks at noon and at sunset; he paints them in snow, in fine weather, on an overcast day, and so on. The same is true of a line of poplars, or of Rouen Cathedral. In 1890 he wrote to his friend Gustave Geffroy, "I'm hard at it, working stubbornly on a series of different effects (grain stacks), but at this time of year the sun sets so fast that it's impossible to keep up with it. . . ."[6]

The preacher who takes seriously the transcendent in the midst will find even greater difficulty in "keeping up with" God's presence in the world. We are called not just to be a mouth for the Lord, but also an eye for the Lord, watching and witnessing to God's activity in the world around us.

But is there any evidence, beyond the committed opinions of religious people, that transcendence in the midst is being experienced today? Alister Hardy was Linacre Professor of Zoology at Oxford University. In 1969 he founded the Religious Experience Research Unit and was its first director from 1969 to 1976. His book, *The Spiritual Nature of Man*, records the remarkable response the Unit received.[7] An initial gathering of four thousand firsthand accounts led to the conclusion that, "a large number of people even today possess a deep awareness of a benevolent nonphysical power which appears to be partly or wholly beyond, and far greater than, the individual self."[8] He goes on:

> At certain times in their lives many people have had specific, deeply felt transcendental experiences which have made them all aware of the presence of this power. The experience when it comes has always been quite different from any other type of experience they have ever had. They do not necessarily call it a religious experience, nor does it occur only to those who belong to an institutional religion or who indulge in corporate acts of worship. It often occurs to children, to atheists and agnostics, and it usually induces in the person concerned a conviction that the everyday world is not the whole of reality: that there is another dimension to life.[9]

Alister Hardy's work has been carried on by David Hay and others. David Hay notes that although Western cultures discourage bold claims of a religious nature, when encouraged, people stand firm by their positive response to the question, "Have you ever been aware of or influenced by a presence or power, whether you call it God or not, which is different from your everyday self."[10] Hay is now working to show that the phenomenology of religious experience is being neglected by modern scientific thinkers in a way that produces a distorted understanding of a "widespread and normal field of human experience."[11]

 In these terms, the preacher becomes more than an observer of God's presence. The preacher becomes an advocate of a reality otherwise being neglected in the Western world with its overrationalized culture. The task of the pulpit becomes a witness to the reality of transcendence in the midst, which will broaden life and our perception of it. Like the radio operator receiving messages covertly under a reactionary regime where news is controlled, the preacher is identifying realities otherwise neglected or ignored in our culture. Or like the astronomer, looking at the same sky as those who stand in the crowd, the preacher sees what is there but not necessarily perceived by others who simply see "stars," which to the astronomer are the Bear or the Plough.

In such a context the preacher becomes more than an observer. The role now involves the preacher in being an interpreter. From the pulpit people should expect not only to hear what the preacher, and those whom the preacher quotes have seen and experienced, with an indication of their meaning. They need also to have identified that which they themselves are experiencing, with the necessary help to interpret it. Like the Ethiopian eunuch whom Philip the evangelist met, our congregations need some help in understanding what they read (Acts 8:26-31). He had been overtaken by an experience he couldn't understand. With not a little difficulty, Philip got alongside the Ethiopian and helped him to grasp the significance of what he read. The preacher's task is no less than that.

The size of the task is suggested by imagining the variety of experiences people who sit in the pew on any given Sunday have brought with them! Internal questions and affirmations, family relationships, work experiences, abilities and disabilities, hopes and fears, riches or poverty, surrounded by friends or largely alone, the list goes on. Yet, in the context of worship, and with Bible in hand, the preacher's privilege is so to expound and witness to the transcendent God who is in our midst that each may recognize and enter into the meaning in his or her situation. There can be few higher privileges than drawing alongside so many people at that intimate level that changes lives for the better.

So the preacher is observer who sees and witnesses, and interpreter who draws alongside to make sense of where people are.

"Where people are" is not a simple matter, however. So far we have thought largely of personal and individual elements of human experience. But "where people are" also relates to a wider setting than personal, family, and local life. The media age ensures that the context for everyone of us is in the whole wide world. Our congregations bring with them the news they have seen on television or heard on radio or read in the newspaper. Is the transcendent in the midst there, also? If so, how do we make our witness on that larger stage?

A variety of attempts have been made to grapple with the issue of how God is present in the world. That question is made all the more complicated because of the influence of the Enlightenment, with its emphasis on human reason, and the scientific revolution and enterprise that was built on it. How can God act in any free way when the world God made seems to answer to certain basic principles sometimes referred to as scientific laws?

Many in our congregations may not, of course, have viewed the question in that academically elevated light (though probably many more have than we preachers tend to allow). But few can avoid the question "Why?" about many things that happen in life. Why did certain people die young when others lived so long? Why do some people seem to make dramatic recoveries from illness and others do not? Why do natural disasters happen? Why does good not always seem to be rewarded in life, or evil punished? At any given time there are probably three or four items in the news, and three or four more in our personal experiences, that reinforce the questions. Where is the transcendent in the midst on all these occasions?

Maurice Wiles expressed the difficulties involved in arguing for a day by day detailed involvement of God in the world's activities. Instead he claimed that:

> We can make best sense of this whole complex of experience and of ideas if we think of the whole continuing creation of the world as God's one act, an act in which he allows radical freedom to his human creation. The nature of such creation . . . is incompatible with the assertion of further particular divinely initiated acts within the developing history of the world. [12]

By emphasizing the single work of God as a continuing creation, Wiles encourages us to search out the purposes and intentions of God's creative work. By discerning these we will be on the way to recognizing what God is doing in the world in that general way. All that coheres with that purpose will therefore be God's activity, since they fit in with the purpose for which God made (and makes) the world.

In such a setting we need to ask about our understanding of biblical teaching about creation and redemption, about destiny and freedom, about chance and necessity. Our reading both of science and of history becomes significant, too, since they provide material for reading back the degree to which, and the events in which, the purposes of God for the world were either fulfilled or opposed. What is more, the understanding of this whole process receives a particular focus and interpretation in the ministry of Jesus Christ. Wiles argues:

> This then is the fashion of God's acting in the world . . . making possible the emergence, both individually and corporately, of a genuinely free human recognition and response to what is God's intention in the creation of the world.[13]

In the context of our approach in this chapter, therefore, we help our hearers to recognize the transcendent in the midst wherever they see God's purposes for the world being worked out.

There is a crucial question remaining, however, about the part we may play in cooperating with God in the world: How may our lives do more than witness to transcendence in the midst?

David Jenkins addresses this question. [14] He, too, is reluctant to speak of "interventionist" acts of God in a world whose story is told in terms of critical historical study and rigorous scientific method. He does concentrate serious attention, however, on the question of how we recognize God's work, and what part we may play in it. He views God's work in creation, what followed in the story of the people of Israel, and story of Jesus Christ, as the significant basis for human involvement in the development of the continuing story. He sees the kingdom of God as a focusing context for understanding this perception.

> The kingdom of God is the focusing symbol of a faith and claim that the life of men and women and the history of humankind can be made sense of within a story because the universe itself is part of that story. This story is the story of God's risking creation so that he may share love in the establishing of a kingdom, a city, a promised land or a shared and shareable space, with persons or beings who are capable of relationships with him and yet are other than himself.[15]

For Christians this means that:

> To discover that Jesus . . . is the Christ (which is what, for Christians, the resurrection is all about) is to discover that in enabling the story, in taking part in the story, and in steadfastly contributing to making the story come true, God pursues the ways of immanence, identification, service and suffering which are a severe affront to the normal, or indeed normative, human ideas of power.[16]

On this basis, the preacher is doing more than enabling others to recognize the presence of transcendence in the midst. We are issuing a call to involvement, to perceiving God's action in the world and being engaged in it. Using the model of the Kingdom makes the parables available as guides to God's presence among us. So does the use of the biblical stories as our stories. So does the reference to God's ways being different from the world's ways. The preacher has become not only witness and interpreter, the preacher is now *prophet*.

Yet we may still ask whether we have done justice to the nature of God's presence in the midst. Is it enough to testify to the ways in which transcendence breaks in upon us; to interpret what that means in the lives of individuals; and to point to God's purposes in creation to the present day, focused on Jesus and recognized in terms of the Kingdom being established?

We may not yet have made proper room for God's own freedom to act within history. Wiles and Jenkins safeguard the integrity of the scientifically understood universe. Why would a God who made it thus interfere with it in any other way? The question is well put. But is it in itself not too limited a question? To be more precise, is it not too limited to the domain of reason and logic?

John Habgood makes this point with all the more authority, since he is himself a distinguished scientist.

> We do not break the laws of nature every time we act freely or create something new. But neither do the laws, the regularities, say everything that is to be said about freedom and creativity. The universe, in other words, seems to be open-textured. Each of us knows at least one place, in our own hearts and wills, where what happens is open to being influenced by personal decision.[17]

Once we can break through to that realization, that God is not controlled by such laws as we feel ourselves to have discovered, then spiritual freedom and perception also break through. So, in relation to prayer, Habgood can write:

> Prayer is the exploration of that freedom, both God's and ours. It is the sending of our spirits beyond the realm of calculations, necessities and regularities, to the realm of openness with God and openness to God, where God's freedom to give or to withhold is openly and gladly acknowledged.[18]

The preacher who is witness of the divine presence, interpreter of God's presence in individual lives, and prophet of God's activity in the world has become also *the herald of liberation,* declaring that the transcendent in the midst is not bound. God may be perceived anywhere, since God is free to be everywhere.

2

Cultivated or Salvaged

Creation and Redemption

Traditionally the Catholic side of christendom has stressed Creation, Incarnation, and Sacrament, whereas the Protestant preacher has stressed Redemption, Atonement, and the Word.

The emphasis on the Creation has clear consequences. It is affirmative of the world. It sees the world as God's gift, and therefore wishes to be positive about it at every point. The church seeks to be at home in the culture, and to embrace as much of the cultural life around it as possible. It has even been a traditional Catholic missionary principle to baptize entire communities into the faith. It has tended not so much to oppose other religious ways it has found traditionally among a people, but rather to try to gather them into the newfound faith under the Catholic wing. It sees the Incarnation as affirming human life, rather than revealing its weaknesses. It also sees the Incarnation as an offering of life up to God, as something worth presenting. If it needs a particular image of the church, it would be the church as salt, mixed among the layers of food in order to preserve it, rather than distinct from the food seeking to influence it. The result is that the Catholic emphasis upon Creation, Incarnation, and Sacrament plays down the difference between the church and the culture in which it is set.

The strength of this position is that it affirms an essential continuity between nature and grace. It does not see them as two separate worlds that somehow have to be offered as alternatives. It does not seek to gather converts out of one into the other. It sees them as concentric circles, but having a lot of common area between them. As such, the demands upon the Christians about being different are much less burdensome than can be the case with Protestants.

The weaknesses are that it is difficult from such a position to demonstrate the distinctiveness of the Christian experience as such. This may be why in the Roman Catholic Church there is strong emphasis on what ought to be done in relation to the church; as in attending Confession, coming to Mass, and on the place and authority of the priesthood and the clerical hierarchy. It is also difficult to place proper emphasis upon human sinfulness when one is trying to highlight the essential goodness of creation and culture. Neither is it, from a biblical point of view, easy to account for the inordinate amount of space given to the Passion of Jesus Christ in the gospel.

The Protestant emphasis has tended to come in from the other side, on Redemption, the Atonement, and the Word. It sees the world as infected in every part by sinfulness. (This does not mean that everything is sinful, but rather that every part of humanity has been somehow made less than the best by the virus called sin.) It is therefore suspicious of the world and of culture, and can easily be reluctant to be involved in cultural activities because of their danger. The relation to the world is dominated by the desire to convert it, rather than to affirm it. There is great stress on the distinctiveness of the church as a different entity altogether. Converts tend to be gathered out of the world into the church, and in many cases this has the result that the church life takes over almost all the nonworking and nonsleeping time of church members. If there is a single image that defines the church from this point of view, it is likely to be light in the darkness, or a city set on a hill.

The redemption approach places strong emphasis on the Barthian idea of an *essential discontinuity between nature and grace.* There is no way that men or women can get themselves from one to the other, or even slide unknowingly from one to the other. If there is a crisis situation then one has to decide, not necessarily once only but again and again, about being "spiritual" rather than "worldly."

The strength of this position is that the challenge of the gospel to unbelievers is clear-cut. There is a sharp distinction between world and church. The choice to be made is a choice that moves the person out of one context into another. Converts therefore know they are converts, and know where they are. They find themselves in the new family of the church, often leaving behind the friendships that they've had before.

The weakness of this position is that new converts may feel themselves at home in the church, but can also feel themselves distinctly away from home whenever they are not in the church. Important areas of life, like daily work, can easily be seen as activity in an alien land. Links with previous friends can be weakened, thus also weakening the possibility of influencing them for the faith. And there is a tendency to spiritualize life to the neglect of social and political issues as being part of Christian discipleship.

Are these two positions necessarily alternatives? In John's Gospel, chapter twelve, there is the story of some Greeks asking to see Jesus. His response is wholly unexpected. He says "The hour has come for the Son of Man to be glorified" (a thought previously held back in John's telling of the story). It is a most significant moment in the unfolding of John's Gospel. Jesus goes on to outline the basis of his work, something for which his disciples had been eagerly awaiting: "Unless a grain of wheat falls into the earth and dies, it remains just a single grain; but if it dies, it bears much fruit." Whatever can this mean, especially as a centerpiece of the kingdom of God?

John's Gospel says it was Passover time, which means that they were getting ready for the forty days preceding Pentecost, the Jewish harvest festival, and their focus was on their crops. Jesus was reminding them of the simple lesson of death and resurrection that is written everywhere into Creation, from the crops, through the generations, and into the stars. Dying and rising are common features of the world God has made. Jesus then goes on to point out that death and resurrection is the way he also must take. He is the seed who will be put into the ground and buried, but who will by resurrection produce the new harvest, the people of God, the Body of Christ. Then he adds a third point. In verses 25 and 26, Jesus makes it clear that anyone who wants to be a disciple must go via the same pattern of death and resurrection. It is a harmonious feature of Creation, Calvary, and Christianity. By putting these three things together, Jesus joins Creation and Redemption in himself.

If we take Creation seriously, alongside Redemption, and see them as two parts of the one saving activity of God, then certain things follow with great clarity.

The first is that the uniqueness of Jesus becomes more significant, not less. It means that elements like death and resurrection are not invented by him or for him. His experience of them is made unique only because he is unique. It is precisely because he is so different from the rest of us that his dying and rising can be the basis of liberation for us all. We need have no fears for the importance of Jesus when we stress Creation. Rather we begin to see him in his true light, as the Word of Creation as well as of Redemption.

There is a much broader second point to make, however. Christians need not and must not be dismissive of good deeds, beautiful attitudes, and truthful discoveries made outside the church. These are the footprints of God in the world. Anything that is good and beautiful and true must come from God. Good can have no other source than God. We need not therefore resist these things in culture. We need rather to embrace them as part of our inheritance as the children of God.

Thomas Aquinas taught that the human search for beauty, love, and truth is in reality a search for God. This is so because God made us to be seekers in this way. But the really deep perception of Aquinas was that as we, seeking love, beauty, and truth, unknowingly seek God, it is also God's way of seeking us. This means that our attitude to those who are not Christian, but are clearly culturally developed, is not, "You may be . . . but you also need to be converted," but rather "Because you are . . . you will want to know the one who gave you these gifts." It makes all the difference to our evangelism.

In the third place, we have to be more willing to recognize Kingdom signs out in the world beyond the boundaries of the church, not least in the most unexpected people. I wonder, for example, whether Bob Geldof was not a sign of the kingdom, when he took the initiative over the people starving in Ethiopia, and gathered the young people of the world together to do something about it, while telling governments what he thought of them because of their delay? I would want to say the same about Mikhail Gorbachev, who through *glasnost* and *perestroika* opened the way to a whole new development in the world. To affirm these people is not necessarily to say they are Christians. It is rather to acknowledge that God is somehow working through the truth that they perceive and the commitment they offer. It is for Christians to recognize these putative signs of the Kingdom and stand beside them and affirm what they are doing. (Such people still need themselves to come to know God through Jesus Christ, but they must not be rejected for what they do because they have not yet reached that stage.)

In the fourth place this Creation view means that *we can more easily begin where people are with our biblical preaching, and speak about what they know in language that they understand.* The Wise Men in the story of the birth of Jesus are surely in the gospel story for that very purpose. They make it plain how people could start with purely "secular" knowledge and find their way to Herod's palace. Then they had to decide whether they would accept a revelation from the Scripture about where the princely baby was actually to be born. But their search for truth got them as far as the palace in their own right. Had they not followed that, they would not have got to the point of revelation. Biblical preachers need to lay great store by that insight.

None of the great problems faced by the world will be solved 5. *except by reference to what God has revealed in Jesus Christ.* His life and teaching, his death and resurrection, his ascension, and our hope of his second coming are directly related to starvation and ecology, to racism and deprivation, to war and injustice, to unemployment and genetic engineering. The link is not always obvious, and the biblical preacher will need to know about both subjects. The implication of Jesus as the word of Creation is that what God has revealed through him provides us with the values by which to face the world's problems. People desperately need biblical preachers to make that clear.

Then, sixth, this kind of emphasis means that *there is both* 6. *continuity and discontinuity between nature and grace.* On the one side it is true that men and women cannot simply think their way into the kingdom of God. Our unworthiness is undoubtedly a barrier to that. But in order to affirm our need for God's grace, we don't have to stress absolute discontinuity between nature and grace. If there is no continuity at all, then there is nothing we can say that will be understood; no place we can find people where a conversation will begin; no path back from being lost to being found.

One final reflection, which is in part a personal testimony, 7. is that *we understand the Scriptures better, and find them to be much more deep and resourceful than we imagine, when we subject them to the test of today's big issues.* As long as we use the Bible only for our personal spirituality, and as some kind of guide to our church activity, we narrow down the Bible potential. When we start to expose it, however, to the issues raised above, we begin to see how much more there is than ever we imagined. We also see that some of our interpretations in the past have been too narrow or even misplaced. The Bible becomes a much more exciting and compendious volume when it is read by someone open to all that is happening in the world today.

If biblical preachers will not take up this task, then we may find biblical preaching being pushed to the sidelines of life more and more. We have reached a critical moment in the history of biblical preaching, and only biblical preachers can do something about it.

3

Doctrine as a Rhythm for Life

Dying and Rising with Jesus

The trouble with Christian doctrine is that it comes to us in creedal statements. As such, it is written down, formally constructed, and historically sanctified. If it is the basis for catechesis, it seems to be fixed and immobile. We receive it from the past, and treat it with respect and even veneration now.

That is a good tradition, with strong scriptural basis. Paul defends his own status as an apostolic preacher in such terms. "For I handed on to you as of first importance what I in turn received: that Christ died for our sins in accordance with the scriptures, and that he was buried, and that he was raised on the third day in accordance with the scriptures" (1 Cor. 15:3-4). Paul's introductory words in that passage are heavy with the sense of a tradition received, cherished, and passed on as received. The Christian church needs such continuity of commitment and belief. It comes to us in our Christian journey like the lines on the highway that identify the road.

But we must not limit the value of doctrine to establishing our faithful links with the past.

The primitive instinct to preserve tradition by reiteration was obliged to give way to the perceived need to continue its history by restatement and interpretation. The dynamicism of the New Testament traditions concerning Jesus was compromised through such a process of preservation in that this process involves petrification, trapping something that was once living in a static form as a fossil might be preserved in a rock or a fly captured.[1]

The analogy of lines on the highway is apt because doctrine provides guidance as to the direction we should take. It is not intended to be a dead deposit from the past but a lively contribution to our future. It signals a journey so far faithfully completed. It also points us to our forward way. When doctrine comes to life in the church, the world should look out!

The challenge to the preacher is that doctrine only comes to life in sermons as it is seen clearly to relate to life. John Stott quotes the great theologian Karl Barth concerning his struggle as a pastor.

I sought to find my way between the problem of human life on the one hand and the content of the Bible on the other. As a minister I wanted to speak to the people in the infinite contradiction of their life, but to speak the no less infinite message of the Bible, which was as much of a riddle as life. Often enough these two magnitudes, life and the Bible, have risen before me (and still rise!) like Scylla and Charybdis: if these are the whence and whither of Christian preaching, who shall, who can, be a minister and preach? [2]

Who indeed? The New Testament does, however, contain examples that may help preachers in the task of setting doctrine free to change lives—ours and those who hear us.

One biblical approach is to bring what is believed into direct relation to life as it is lived by the hearers and readers. Jesus is the supreme example of such a method. He went from place to place, not knowing who he would meet or what he would be asked or what situation he would face. Yet again and again he began where the other person was, individually or in crowds, and related the good news to that situation. As the Archbishop of Canterbury has put it:

Jesus taught also with a wonderful attractiveness. What an amazing teacher he must have been! Not for him the technique of spinning webs of theological intricacy, the tedious homilies which obscured truth from the ignorant and the illiterate. It would seem that most of his teaching was spontaneous, arising from personal encounters with people, responding to their questions, challenges and needs. [3]

So a woman who tells Jesus all about her illness and need is told that faith has made her well (Mark 5:34); and a woman who anoints Jesus' feet with oil is told that her loving action has embraced the forgiveness she evidently needed (Luke 7:47-48). The expression of doubt and puzzlement by the disciple Thomas receives the momentous response from Jesus "I am the way, and the truth, and the life. No one comes to the Father except through me" (John 14:6). A request for some help on praying produces a prayer full of doctrinal weight, yet couched in the simplest of language—the prayer that unites all Christians to this day (Luke 11:2-4).

The same principle is at work in the rest of the New Testament beyond the Gospels. In an attempt to address the problem of a largely slave readership, Peter turns to the very heart of the Christian faith. Encouraging them in their experience of unjust suffering, he writes of Jesus: "He himself bore our sins in his body on the cross, so that, free from sins, we might live for righteousness; by his wounds you have been healed" (1 Pet. 2:24). The solution to their problem of slavery was the atoning death of the Savior of the world!

James uses a deep perception of God's sovereignty in the world to instruct his readers on how they ought to treat the poor (James 2:1-7). To counteract discouragement and half-heartedness, the writer to the Hebrews expounds the depths of Christology. Jesus is "crowned with glory and honor" so that he might "taste death for everyone," and in so doing he was made "perfect through sufferings" (Heb. 2:9-10).

Perhaps the classic case of the use of fundamental doctrines in relation to everyday life is Paul's use of an ancient Christian hymn, in his letter to the church at Philippi. As far as we can tell, the Philippian church was—in Paul's judgment—doing better than most of the others to whom he wrote. He refers to them as those, "whom I love and long for, my joy and crown" (Phil. 4:1). Yet there is obviously at least one thing troubling Paul about them: they can't get along with one another. He wants to be assured that they are "standing firm in one spirit" (Phil. 1: 27). He wants them to be "one in spirit" and purpose, doing " . . . nothing from selfish ambition or conceit, but in humility regard others as better than yourselves" (Phil. 2:2-3). He warns them against "murmuring and arguing" (Phil. 2:14). And there is the particular case of Euodia and Syntyche, who apparently couldn't get along with each other (Phil. 4:2).

Paul's solution to this problem of relationships is not an exhortation on the need to pull together, or the strength of working as a team, or even their need for one another's gifts. He attempted to solve their problem of human relationships by a profound exposition of who Jesus Christ is, and of what he did in giving himself for the salvation of everyone (Phil. 2:5-11). The theological implications of the exposition continue to challenge New Testament scholars. But the use of this passage in Paul's pastoral ministry to the Philippians is clear. For a solution to their problems of relating to one another, they should look to the heart of their faith. The dying and rising of Jesus is the clue to their getting along with one another, if they would accept: "Let the same mind be in you that was in Christ Jesus" (Phil. 2:5). The death, resurrection, and ascension of Jesus are the model for human relationships! The solution to a peripheral pastoral problem is a fundamental theological doctrine.

When preachers take the process seriously, namely that our doctrines are meant to provide the rhythm for Christian living, a number of requirements are laid upon us.

One is that taking the experience of our congregations seriously is not merely advisable, it is vital. As Jesus spoke his word according to the individual or audience he was addressing, and Paul and the other New Testament writers sent letters dealing with the circumstances, hopes, problems, and concerns of their readers, so the modern preacher must take the current experience of the hearers with great seriousness. It is an interesting exercise to delete from the Gospels all reference to the people with whom Jesus was dealing, and then see how much sense one can make of his words or actions! How would that test affect our preaching?

This requirement does not move the center of our content or our authority away from the Bible. But it does guide us in our sensitivity to which message from the Bible will be more appropriate on any given occasion. And it makes it much more likely that the hearers will not only listen but actually embrace what they hear, because it is addressing their lives as they are. As Ralph and Gregg Lewis put it:

> Human experience doesn't become the basis of our message, but it can validate what we're saying; it can punctuate the Word in a way our people will readily understand. Such references to common life become more than application points at the end of the sermon; they serve as guideposts along the way, all pointing to the truth at the end of the road.[4]

I recall speaking at a large conference on the dying and rising of Christ, as Paul expounds it in Romans 6 in relation to baptism. I suggested that the dying and rising was not simply a historical process in the experience of Jesus. Nor is it finally located for us in our moment of baptism. It is also a daily experience of dying to all that Jesus died to, and rising to all that he rose to. He died to everything that opposes God, demeans humanity, frustrates God's purposes, and denies the Kingdom. We are to die to all of that, too. He rose to everything that honors God, elevates humanity, fulfills God's purposes, and establishes the Kingdom.

A week later I received a letter from a woman who had been at that conference. She had gone home and attended Sunday morning church, only to find there another woman whose very sharp tongue she often found most hurtful and destructive.

Instead of doing what she normally did—that is—to boil over inwardly in anger and resentment, but try not to say anything she'd later regret—she went home, knelt at her bedside and asked that she might die to the resentment and anger she felt, and rise to understand and forgive. She wrote to tell me that the death and resurrection had taken place! She hoped I would go on telling people to die and rise with Christ! Both the dying and rising of Christ, and her own baptism, had taken on a new meaning for her in relation to her daily living by faith.

Family life in the light of our understanding of God as trinity, action for the needy in the light of incarnation, commitment to changing society and establishing new beginnings on a basis of the miracles, living by a different set of values in relation to Christ's death and resurrection, and experience of a power that enables one to live by reason of the gift of Pentecost—all are points of direct contact between basic doctrine and daily living. The more the preacher explores doctrinal content in the face of the opportunities and challenges of modern life, the deeper and more profound that doctrinal content will be seen to be, and the more relevant and exciting the preaching task becomes. Far from being dull, preaching with doctrinal emphasis can be most liberating. As Paul Althaus put it, "People today are not tired of preaching, but tired of *our* preaching."[5]

The lively relevance of Christian doctrine stretches far beyond the rather narrow confines of how Christians live their lives, important though that is. It raises the far larger question of how Christian "knowledge" relates to all other forms of knowledge.

There was a time in the history of the church when this was not a problem. At the beginning of this millennium, theology steadily asserted itself as "the queen of the sciences." All other knowledge had theology as its point of reference. All knowledge was God-centered. The Renaissance, with its concentration on human life; the Reformation (oddly enough) with its championing of individual freedom in matters of religion; and the Enlightenment, with its confidence in human reason, have changed all that. As one writer has put it:

> It is still possible for Christians to *impose* comfortable patterns of meaning on the world about them, but the world has meanwhile found a pattern of its own. a language independent of theological assumptions. The world talks back to the theologian. It resists his attempt to speak for it, and to tell it what it should be thinking. There is little echo of the theologian's language in the vocabulary of modern economics, politics or technology. If there is to be any unity of faith and life for the Christian . . . that unity must be generated from *within* a renewed Christian community, as a direct implication of a new understanding of the gospel. The church, in short, can no longer borrow its wholeness from the world around it: *it must bring that wholeness into being itself.*[6]

It is difficult to see how this wholeness will ever be created, communicated, and accepted by the people, unless the preachers comprehend and commend it.

To do so, we preachers have to accept the fact that we are not protected by church walls from the realities that lie beyond them. After all, we, and our congregations, spend most of our time on the other side of those walls. If worship is, as most of us would surely accept, a celebration of all of life under God, then our preaching must somehow take all of life into account. For "the individual with whom I am speaking," or "the audience I am addressing," read "the world in which I live" as the preacher's context. John Wesley's claim to the Bishop of Bristol, "I look upon the whole world as my parish," could perhaps provide the basis for the preacher's motto, "I look upon the whole world as my audience."

How does this work when we seek to relate our doctrinal knowledge to all the other knowledge claims in the world today?

We begin by recognizing that different ways of knowing are necessary for different kinds of knowledge. If a chemist tells you that certain chemicals, when mixed and heated, produce an explosion, she is talking about what she can demonstrate to be the case. If you don't agree with the chemist, she will provide you with the chemicals and the means of heating, beat a hasty retreat, and allow you to carry out your very last experiment! For that kind of scientific proof can be openly demonstrated again and again to everyone's satisfaction. But how does a historian know about the fact and the date of Julius Caesar's invasion of Britain? Certainly not by reproducing it every time someone inquires! It depends on monuments, archaeological finds, written documents, maps, and a good deal of making as much sense as possible of limited evidence. How does one make a judgment about whether a piece of music is good? It certainly doesn't depend on scientific matters like how straight the lines are, or how spherical the circles. Nor does it depend on history, as in "Mozart wrote it so it must be good." There are other tests of good music, some objective, many subjective, but all adding up to a genuine claim to knowledge. To move further across the spectrum, how does a general know that his troops will follow him into battle, even to death? If he has demonstrated that scientifically, then he won't have any troops left! What does that knowledge depend on? The general would certainly claim to know. Most of all, what are the ingredients of knowing one is loved. How is that to be demonstrated?

The truth is that each area of knowledge requires a different discipline by which that knowledge is gained. Each is appropriate according to its suitability to discover what needs to be known. No one way may exclude the rest, and no one discipline should be used to discover knowledge for which it is not fitted. I don't want a surgeon telling me he will remove both my kidneys because, although scientifically I can't live without them, he had been reading a poem that suggested the possibility! Each discipline to its own area of knowledge is a fundamental principle.

There is a sharper test, however, that we must apply. Of all the forms of knowledge represented across the spectrum above, from chemist to lover, if one had to choose only one way of knowing and one area of knowledge, where would one go to experience the deepest areas of being human? Would it be to the demonstrable areas of scientific proof, or to the other end where knowledge depends much more on values and on risk—on hope, trust, loyalty, and reverence? The different disciplines are not in watertight compartments. Each draws on some of the others, but the experience of humanity and what it means to be distinctively human relies most heavily on that which is not once-for-all demonstrable but involves trust and hope and vulnerability.

The preacher has the privilege of showing those who will listen that faith, and the knowledge that we claim by faith and that we encapsulate in our doctrine, depends on the different disciplines in the spectrum above. It relies on the consistency of the universe that is at the heart of modern science. It counts on historical evidence concerning Israel, Jesus and his disciples, and the growth of the early church. It involves subjective judgments about values and issues. It includes intuitive trust of other people. And it leads inexorably into the vulnerability and commitment of trusting one's life without proof, but in the belief that this vulnerable commitment is the best way of making sense of all the evidence, external and internal.

One can go further. It isn't simply that Christian doctrine uses all the spectrum of disciplines but puts most trust in the "values" end of that spectrum. It is rather that Christian believing turns the spectrum into journey, a road, a path to be traveled. It is like the track followed by the longjumper. The path has meaning and validity in itself, but its ultimate purpose is to transcend itself by enabling someone to launch beyond the path into a different way of traveling altogether.

Other ways of knowing need not be in opposition to faith knowledge. Indeed they provide part of the journey. It is only as they lock us into themselves—as in "I'm a scientist so I can't accept that God created the world" or "I'm a Christian so I have to accept the six-day creation story"—that two paths to knowledge become mutually exclusive. The faith claim is that all authenticated knowledge is to be accepted and affirmed, but that faith-knowing launches us into the areas of the "transcendent in the midst" and points us way beyond what human reason alone can achieve.

Our basis for this kind of claim is our belief about Jesus Christ as the Word become flesh, referred to in the previous chapter. If this claim is true, then this is the focal point around which everything else revolves. As such it may be translated into any discipline and any terminology. A Christian gynecologist put it like this, writing of Jesus Christ as the Word of Creation:

> Jesus is Lord. It is he by whom all things exist. It is he who spiralled the DNA helix, who choreographed the genetic quadrille in cell division, who scored the hormonal symphony, and who heals the wounds we bind up . . . and by looking to this Lord, the doctor of Galilee, this sustainer of every galaxy, we can day by day calibrate our behaviour.[7]

The language is dramatic, but the point is clear. If Jesus Christ is the Word of creation as well as the Lord of redemption, then his place may be affirmed at the center of all that is. To put it another way:

We live in a world where knowledge is fragmented, but the problems we have to face are not. The problems are all interrelated. Scientists can no longer duck away from ethical issues. Engineers have to consider environment. Historians can't ignore economics. Theologians have to come to terms with biology. And so on, and so on. And the most pressing political, social and economic problems of today's world have all these dimensions and more. Knowledge conceived of as isolated blocks of material is not only ineffective but false to reality.[8]

The challenge of this reality is not that the preacher should somehow be an expert in all these areas. But it is to recognize that in our congregations there are usually people who are involved in these areas of life, either as experts or as those who, one way or another, are on the receiving end. We are not called to give learned lectures on all these areas of knowledge. Indeed we are specifically required not to do so! But our listeners can expect a message that is both sufficiently deep in its theological content, and sufficiently broad in its embrace of the world in its present life, that hearers will be able to see how the door from the church leads directly into their daily experience. They will make the rest of the journey in the strength of God's word to them.

A final clue to the fulfilment of this task is contained in the Philippians 2 passage on Jesus Christ, that is better seen, not merely as a series of events but as a steady movement through a single ministry from start to finish: Jesus moves from glory to glory via lowly obedient suffering love that is raised and glorified. To see this only as a series of saving events (which of course it is) is to limit its meaning and power. It is also a single divine act in Jesus Christ, an act that is the basis of the Kingdom, the ground of our salvation, and the rhythm for our life in Christ. This is why it can so easily apply to the particular circumstances of the church at Philippi.

The preacher must proclaim doctrine, not as a series of trophies in cabinets—to be described, observed, praised, and commended—but as living realities, accounting for the fundamental truths that lie at the heart of our faith; and also reaching out to engage all the realities around us.

This does not mean that we are free to change our doctrine in the light of modern fashion. As Lesslie Newbigin observed about the resurrection of Jesus Christ: "The simple truth is that the resurrection cannot be accommodated in any way of understanding the world except one of which it is the starting point."[9] We are not to address modern situations, problems, and people in a way that trims the sails of theological truths to the wind of popular opinion. Rather Christian doctrine reaches out with loving hands to bring new life and meaning where people are.

That this will take time, effort, and skill on the part of the preacher is beyond doubt. Eddie Askew tells the story of the artist who with twelve deft strokes created a sketch. When asked by an admirer how long it took to do, he replied, "About thirty years!" Askew then comments that however skilled we are, "Without the practice, the discipline and the sweat, the talent is only a promise."[10] Every preacher will say "Amen" to that.

4

Atonement, Repentance, and Conversion
If This is the Solution, What is the Problem?

The cross of Jesus Christ is central to the Christian gospel.[1] This means that the doctrine of the Atonement is central also. Evangelicals have, quite properly, never limited our view to one doctrine of the Atonement.[2] But we have defended strongly any that *are* clearly based in Scripture. This has been necessary against the opposition, at times, of more liberal theology; particularly where the ideas of substitution, or even sacrifice, were expounded from our pulpits in relation to the death of Jesus, and met with opposition on theological, philosophical, or moral grounds.

The strength of this defense of the traditional theories of atonement has been considerable. Despite the arguments of more liberal scholars, it remains clear that the elements of sacrifice, and indeed of substitution, are present in the words used by New Testament writers, and were part of their intention.[3] Theologically, these cases are defensible in terms of the nature of God, God's relationship to the world, the experience of human rebellion against God, and the need for an adequate way in which that rebellion may change into love and service.[4] There is also strong experiential grounds. Various people at various times have needed one or other of these ways in which they may be assured that the approach to God is available to them. The fact that in a particular age or culture a certain rational approach is most popular provides no ground for denying that approach in other ages or cultures. It is significant that the debate about the nature of the Atonement has quietened down after the staunch defense of traditional theories over a number of decades.

In all this discussion and defense, our case has been that we were against narrowing down the meaning of the death of Jesus. We have, I believe quite rightly, argued that a variety of theories of the Atonement was necessary, provided they were based on scriptural evidence, because there is a variety of needs represented in the human heart and mind, and different theories of the Atonement have met that variety as a single one could not. In this context we have defended the cross as the extent to which God's love would go; as the sign and place of God's victory over evil; as the place where Jesus as our representative did for us what we cannot do for ourselves; as the supreme example of sacrifice, offered by the unique High Priest who was also the sacrifice, on our behalf; and as the place where Jesus actually stood in for us, so that we might find our way back to God.

In addition to defending those theories of the Atonement, which were believed to be based in the Scripture, evangelical Christians have tended also to be critical of other theories of the Atonement that were not seen to be in harmony with the total scriptural message. Coming to this category have been the works of McCleod Campbell looking at the father/son relationship as the motif for understanding;[5] the views of Horace Bushnell, using vicarious sacrifice;[6] the relationship model of R. C. Moberley;[7] and the vast exposition by F. W. Dillistone,[8] using the idea of alienation as a recurring pattern throughout history, and of self-giving as the way in which it is dealt with. To a greater or lesser extent, such views have come under evangelical criticism.

The danger is, I fear, that in arguing for what we have viewed as adequate views of the Atonement, based on the Scripture and defending them against that which was considered inadequate, we may have narrowed down the possible understanding of the death of Jesus. It may be that we have hindered the development of new theories of the

Atonement, which would be equally based on the Scripture as those doctrines from the past that we have accepted, but also wholly apposite for our situation in today's world. After all, when Anselm, Luther, Calvin, and Aulen produced their theories of the Atonement, they were in harmony with the prevailing thought of the day in one way or another. What I am feeling for is new understanding of the Atonement of Jesus that is equally related to our situation today.

There is perhaps an even greater reason for making this attempt than that we should try to be obviously relevant to our modern culture. It is that fundamental to all understanding of the death of Jesus Christ has been its place as a solution to a problem. A verse from Cecil Frances Alexander's hymn, "There was no other good enough, to pay the price of sin; He only could unlock the gates of heaven and let us in" may be too crude for many people, but it puts its finger right on the spot. Even the more gentle views of the meaning of the death of Jesus, like that of Abelard, seeing it as a demonstration of the love of God, does not give the impression that it need not have happened. A regular appearance of the small Greek word meaning "must" in the Gospel of Mark is a subtle yet obvious reminder that in the gospel there lies the necessity of the death of Jesus. To say that it was necessary only given the circumstances of the day, or of human nature, does not take the point away. The way Mark records Jesus, early in his Gospel, as talking about the bridegroom being taken away; and then in the middle of the Gospel turning the whole story round with a series of statements about the necessity of going to Jerusalem, and of being put to death, all underlines the same point. The death of Jesus Christ is, both biblically and theologically, a necessary solution to an urgent problem.[9]

That problem is human sinfulness. Whether the death of Jesus is seen as a demonstration of God's love meant to soften hard hearts, or a price paid as a way of averting God's justice, or a sacrifice made willingly on behalf of the rest, or the crucial battle in the war against evil, or the bearing by Jesus in his own body of the results of our evil that we could not bear in ours, at every stage the problem is sin and sinfulness, and a solution is via the death of Jesus.

In general, evangelical Christians have sought to approach the matter in that direction. We have defined what we understand sin to be, and then looked to the cross of Jesus as the solution to sin thus defined. By so doing we may have narrowed down our understanding of the cross and its purpose. In this chapter, we will look at it the other way around. We may discover much more about the nature of sin, and of what it means to turn away from sin and lead a different life through Jesus Christ, by asking *what is the nature of the problem of sin, if the death of Jesus Christ is the solution*. This puts us under pressure to make sure that we have adequately understood the various insights into the death of Jesus in the New Testament, not only concerning the meaning of the cross, but also concerning the extent and depth of sin. In doing so, we shall also come to understand more clearly what is the nature of repentance and conversion.

There is no need to expound further the traditional theories of the Atonement, since each has been referred to above, and since all have adequate outlines and defenses. Rather, here, we turn to ways of looking at the meaning of the death of Jesus that may not have been given enough consideration in relation to our present situation in the world. I offer two examples.

The first has to do with the so-called "cry of dereliction." These are the words of Jesus, as he hung on the cross, "My God, my God, why have you forsaken me?" (Mark 15:34; Matt. 27:46). For Christian theologians over the centuries, this has been treated as one of the problem sayings. The meaning of the death of Jesus, namely that in some way he was taking upon himself our sinfulness, or at the very least bearing the consequences of it, was a major premise of all such discussions. So was the conviction that somehow, in dying in this way, Jesus was doing the will of his heavenly father. It has also been accepted that those who put Jesus to death were themselves responsible for what they did. But this cry of dereliction does not fit readily with any of the theories.

Why, for example, if Jesus was doing the will of his father, and had come to do so, did he now offer a cry that suggests that things have taken an unexpected, even an unwelcome, turn? Surely this is the very thing that Jesus is recorded in the different Gospels as prophesying. It was the disciples who found it difficult to accept, even as far as Gethsemane and the Mount of Olives. But Jesus seemed all the way through to know what was coming, to tell them confidently about it, and to be ready for it. Why, now, this complaining cry?

There is a deep theological problem, also. If the oneness of Jesus with his heavenly father is as profound as the Gospel writers in general, and John's Gospel in particular, make plain, how can the word "forsaken" be used? The oneness of father and son within the Trinity is an eternal reality. How can one forsake the other?

The two main solutions offered hardly satisfy the anxiety contained in these questions. The first is that what we have here is a very subtle use of Psalm 22, which Jesus would of course know well, as would the Jewish people around him at the cross. Psalm 22 begins with these very words, known to us as the cry of dereliction. By the end of the psalm, however, the note of forsakenness is replaced by a confidence in God's graciousness. In delivering his people, either Jesus did not manage to get through his quotation of the whole psalm in order to reach the deliverance part, or the use of the psalm at the beginning is an invitation to those who have faith and perception to understand that there is another side to the story. One can only feel that on the one hand it is very odd if the greatest event in the world is somehow mismanaged by God so that God's only son cannot get through to the end of his quotation, and on the other hand this seminal event in the world history being left to a subtle interpretation of an undeclared intention seems rather too vague an approach to such an important issue.

The other solution that is often provided is that though it is impossible to understand the depths of meaning of this cry of dereliction, it reflects the fact that for a brief moment the awful cloud of human sinfulness was such an enormity that even the divine son felt himself to be forsaken by a loving father. In this case, as in the use of Psalm 22 above, there is plainly a great deal of helpfulness in the suggestion. Certainly this explanation is in no danger of playing down the awful significance of the occasion, nor of the unique task that was being undertaken by Jesus. Yet it means that Jesus (on traditional interpretations of his divine nature) was wrong at the deepest point of human history. He couldn't be separated from the father with whom he was one. However helpful the explanation may be psychologically, it does not seem to take us all the way we need to go.

We see things more clearly if we identify the exact context of the cry of dereliction. The two attempts that we have seen to be valuable, though not entirely satisfactory, are seeking to interpret the cry of dereliction in relation to *the ultimate victory of God in Christ over sin.* Without taking away its place in that process, we might do better to look at it rather in the context of the *relationship of God to the suffering that is caused by sin.*

If we take it from that point of view, it is not only unnecessary to have a full explanation of this mystery (as though somehow our salvation is at stake if we don't), rather it is vital that we do not do so. It is the very pointlessness, and inexplicability of so much of the suffering in the world that resulted from sin, which lies at its very heart. That it has its moment of inexplicability, here in the central event of history, is a vital insight into its meaning. We not only need not see the victory as we try to go through this experience, we absolutely must not do so. It is of the essence that it is experienced in its own right.

If this interpretation is anywhere near the truth, then the experience of Christ on the cross is linked to aspects of sinfulness, which over the centuries have been undervalued, or even frankly neglected. There has been a tendency for sin to be understood in individual terms; even individualistic terms. I am responsible for my sins, and answerable to God for them. I must not blame God for effects of my sin in my life. Such basic insights are essential, and there is no wish here to remove these. But we have been less insistent, or clear, regarding the corporate nature of sinning, and concerning the amount of suffering there is in the world that the sufferers have not brought upon themselves, but which has been caused by others.

As to the first, the corporate nature of sin, it is clearly present in the Old Testament, where so much of the story is told in terms of nation against nation. God's blessing and God's wrath come upon nations, as well as upon tribes or families or individuals. In the New Testament there are passages that we, very significantly, find it difficult to handle. There is Jesus' talk about the sheep and goats, and the gathering of the nations together at the end of history (Matt. 25:31-46). There is Paul's wrestling with the nation of the Jews in relation to all other nations (Romans 9–11), and to the way in which somehow all of creation is groaning in connection with the sinfulness of human nature (Rom. 8:18-27). And there is the wonderful picture in Revelation of the end time when people from every nation and every tribe will be worshiping (Rev. 7:9-12).

We struggle with these passages of scripture, not least because the Enlightenment has led us to a highly individual view of human life. Modern emphases on rights, choices, individuality and diversity, which have led in postmodernism to the rejection of categories and roles altogether, make it very difficult for us to grasp these corporate interpretations of sin and sinning.[10]

We have come near to it in some theological reflection on Paul's use of the idea of "principalities and powers" (Eph. 6:10-12). These were originally understood to refer to spiritual forces of evil in the world that seek to dominate human life at every level. More recently, however, some scholars have tended to interpret principalities and powers as meaning those corporate groups who somehow commit themselves to evil activity, to dominating others unjustly, and to seeking to gain for themselves at the expense of others by so dominating them.[11] In modern times Nazi Germany has been seen in this light. Others have seen Communist states in the same way. Still others see capitalism in similar terms. Multinational corporations and conglomerates have sometimes been so portrayed. There is no need, however, for the spiritual interpretation to be set over against this more human and materialistic interpretation.[12] For the one could be operating through the other.

But there may be a deeper level still at which we need to take seriously the corporateness of human sinning. The book of Genesis hints at it. Once Adam and Eve are banished from the garden, the story of humankind takes off as a geometrical progression of sin and evil deeds, which steadily incorporates more and more human beings. It picks up speed through to the flood. Sadly, after the new beginning, a geometrical progression returns. It is the other side of the coin of that mutual dependence and caring for one another that was God's intention for humankind in its creation. We are meant day by day to help in one another's lives, to build one another up, to enrich one another, and to enable one another. There was a geometrical progression intended there, as life became richer and better. To turn that coin over is to introduce the same level of progression, but in entirely the wrong direction.

It is the difference between a spaceship hurtling on its course and a spaceship that has lost its way. The farther the second one goes, the farther it is away from its original purpose, and from its intended course. Neither the speed nor the capacity of the ship will of itself correct the course.

It is this corporate element of suffering, to which each of us contributes, which lies at the heart of so much of the news we see or hear or read today. So many of our modern crises, with all the deaths associated with them—in Africa, Asia, the Middle East, Europe, and Ireland—have their roots in history. The present generations find it difficult to solve the problems because none of them is actually responsible for them. The problems are inherited from a time when no contemporary person was alive, and to which no one can return. Yet the implications and the results, the memories and the pain, have been passed on through the generations.

One can add to this "historical" suffering, a good deal of "contemporary" suffering, in the sense that much of the pain and deprivation being experienced by millions around the world today is not largely the fault of history, but the fault of those of us who are alive today. There truly is no need for there to be a single hungry person in the world. And there is enough space for us all. What is lacking is the will to make the world the kind of place that God intended. None of us wishes it to be thus, but we neither individually nor corporately show the determination to pay the price involved to put it right.[13]

It is precisely here that the cry of dereliction probably has its greatest meaning. It is about God bearing the suffering that we inflict upon one another.

The pointlessness of so much of the suffering in the world, which in a combined way we force on one another, reaches its most poignant level just here: God is a part of the suffering in order to show a better way forward.[14]

This leads to a further theological problem and solution. The problem has to do with a doctrine long held about God, namely, God's impassibility. It was not felt appropriate that God would suffer. But the very oneness of God with Jesus Christ casts doubt on such theology anyway. God does not lose transcendence through this degree of immanence. Rather it is God's transcendent presence in such a setting that gives it its only chance of relief. The God whom we worship is the one who, as Rabbi Hugo Gryn put it about his reaction to losing family in the concentration camps during the last war, "wept with me."

The theological solution offered is far in excess of any problem caused. It is that we have a different perspective on what has always been referred to as "the problem of suffering" in the world. We are no nearer to explaining why suffering is allowed as an element in our daily lives. Nor are we likely ever to be much nearer to that. We have seen how much of it we bring upon ourselves, either individually or corporately. But much more important is the assurance we have that however deep our sense of dereliction may be, God is actually in it with us and the message of the cross is that God is not only in it with us, but that God is actually in it to redeem it. There is no place where we can go on earth's surface where the footsteps of God in Jesus have not preceded us. There is no deep place of suffering where God will not be with us. And God's presence is to redeem.[15]

One begins to understand how deep and significant the message is when one remembers how many millions there are in the world who suffer in one way or another. Our message is not that we do not know how to explain that suffering. It is that too much of it comes from our own wrongdoing; but more important, God is present weeping with those who weep, and God is there in order to bring good out of evil.

There is a significance here for all who seek to follow Jesus Christ. Our commitment must be not only, like God, to seek a world in which there is no suffering, but also to seek to be alongside those who do suffer, not only to share the suffering and offer our sympathy, but also to redeem every suffering situation in the world. It is a challenge to individuals, but it is a corporate challenge also. What it means for our understanding of sin, repentance, and conversion we shall consider below. Here we simply point to the enormous significance of recognizing that the creating and redeeming God both bears our suffering with us, and challenges us to do the same for one another.

We turn now to a second New Testament perception on the death of Jesus that requires much more attention than it has so far received. It is Paul's comment, in the setting of some guidance to the Corinthian Christians about their weekly giving, on the ministry of Jesus: "For you know the generous act of our Lord Jesus Christ, that though he was rich, yet for your sakes he became poor, so that you by his poverty might become rich" (2 Cor. 8:9). Paul is referring not only to the death of Jesus here but also to his entire ministry.[16] Yet the context points unmistakably to the cross because of the use of wealth and poverty as the image. Jesus was not wealthy in the sense of financial wealth either before his birth or after it. The reference to poverty cannot therefore be about his having no money, and leading a modest lifestyle. The wealth that Jesus possessed, his "riches," refer to Paul's vision of him as God's own son. It makes much more sense to see it in terms of the power, the glory, and the majesty that were associated with the presence of God in heaven. It is this that Jesus is seen as leaving behind, in order that we might become rich. And the riches are not physical either, rather they are imagined as the heavenly benefits that God brought to us through Jesus Christ.

If we ask at which point Jesus, from the point of view of his heavenly glory and power, was the most poor, it is plainly the moment of the cross. His poverty to make us rich is his dying for our sins.

If ever there is an understanding of the death of Jesus that is needed today, it is this one. Poverty and riches are two of

—————55

the greatest realities in our world, and the gap between the two forms is one of the world's greatest problems. That the gap is growing between rich and poor makes it even more serious. In this context, the death of Jesus Christ becomes not only spiritual reality in making new life possible for us. It is also a model for behavior; no one who follows Jesus can avoid the challenge to match the generosity of God by being generous themselves in relation the poorest and the neediest. If the cry of dereliction points to God's presence among us in our suffering, Paul's picture in 2 Corinthians reveals the nature of that redemptive work. It is that the wealthy be willing to deny themselves in order that the poor have what they need. The often-repeated statement of Jesus in the Gospels, that those who wished to be his disciples must follow in his steps, takes on deep and poignant signficance at this point (Luke 14:27).[17]

We turn now to the fundamental question with which we began. If so many of the theories of the Atonement that have traditionally dominated the theology of the Church were largely aimed at an individual and individualistic view of sin and its consequences, what is the result of adding these two other images, both much more corporate and biblically based, to our understanding today? Above all what does it add to our proclamation of sin, repentance, and conversion?

About sin, the answer has already emerged from the text. It is that our vision must be enlarged. It was said that Michaelangelo, on one occasion in his studio, had a pupil bring to him a piece of work. The master looked at it for some time, then wrote across it the single Latin word *amplius*. It means "broader, wider." The student would only achieve his aim if he took a much wider perspective. This is the implication of these two texts for our understanding of sinfulness. We are not called to pay any less attention to individual sinfulness and need. But we are called to be clearer about those corporate ways in which sin is conceived and perpetrated, in which suffering is caused, and in which judgment is brought down upon our heads.

This in turn casts clear light on what we understand by repentance. As long as sin is defined solely in individual terms, with equally individual results, repentance can easily be cast in the mold of regret, remorse, and genuine sorrow. Nor is there anything wrong with that way of looking at things. What must be made clear, however, is that repentance is about much more than emotional reflection on our own wrongdoing. The Greek word *metanoia* is not about emotional response. It means a change of mind and involves accepting, as a matter of rational conclusion, that one has been going in the wrong direction, doing the wrong things, and having the wrong attitudes. And it means determining to live differently from now on.

This casts an entirely different light upon our understanding of sin and repentance. For it means that we can no longer say that we feel sorry about the things that we do wrong, but that there is really very little we can do about it. It means that we need to look at structures, at systems, at organizations—including those within the church—in order to discern where corporate sin is at work, where a change of mind is necessary, and where appropriate action should follow. Sin and repentance are given a wider range than simply what goes on in the pulpit and the church and the sanctuary. They become matters for the regional and national governments. When this takes place the categories usually associated with theology become more and more relevant to the life of the nation. By a too narrow view of sin, repentance, and conversion, the church does not primarily deny itself. It denies the world its opportunity to understand what the gospel is about. Understood in this more comprehensive way sin, repentance, and conversion become precisely the categories that enable us to describe many of the realities of contemporary secular events.

It will be for the preacher to make these matters clear. If sometimes our congregations feel that what we say has little to do with their commitments and activities during the week, it may well be because we have been too individualistic in our interpretations. There is no ground for neglecting our challenge to the individual. The personal realities of sin, repentance, and conversion remain as they ever were in relation to the dying of Jesus Christ for our sins. But if our preaching leaves it only at the level of the individual, we may be building up a sense of frustration in relation to the corporate groups to which our hearers belong, in family and society, in work and nation, and at the level of international influence. The broader, corporate view of sin, linked to a properly wide understanding of repentance (changing one's mind) and of conversion (changing one's direction) opens up the whole world scene. Again, for the preacher, it is not about using the pulpit to commend particular schemes of business or theories of politics. But it is about gathering the realities of the life of the world, in health and education, in economics and politics, in employment and poverty, into the framework within which our theological insights operate. If our theology is not deep and extensive enough, it will have nothing to contribute. If we neglect the realities of life around us, then hearers will fail to see the relevance. With both in place, as the hymn writer Edward J. Burns put it, "We have a gospel to proclaim."

5

Reason and Faith

Thinking and Believing

One of the major difficulties faced by preachers is the question about reason and faith. So often in the last century the two have been set over against each other. Reason, in the wake of the Enlightenment, has been used as an argument against the need for faith at all. The human mind is seen as capable, of itself, of observing, identifying, describing, and therefore explaining all that is in the world. Why should we believe what we can eventually prove? On the other side it has often been said that faith is a capacity to perceive what is beyond the reach of reason. Too often it has ended up with a god in the gaps, claiming to know what is not known at present, but with the uneasy feeling that one day it might become known. In cultures that are increasingly dominated by the desire for rational proof, the preacher often feels herself or himself to be caught in that tension and to be occupying a narrower and narrower space.

The aim here is to show that the tension between reason and faith is a necessary one, but that it need not be destructive. It is necessary, because reason is one of God's greatest gifts to humankind. Anything that bypasses our mind is usually, and quite rightly, treated as dangerous. The mind is a receiver and transmitter of truth, the filter through which we receive impressions and make responses. Faith operates, not over against the mind, but on a basis of what the mind can perceive. Faith claims to operate beyond the area within which reason can demonstrate proof, and yet in a way that validates reason as a central human activity.

The tension, however, is not simply two-way. The question of thinking and believing requires a journey that takes in a number of essential elements.

The first is the nature of faith as it is understood in the New Testament.[1] The understanding of faith as a somewhat emotional response to external stimulant does not do justice to the New Testament picture of faith. It is a much more sturdy animal than that! It is varied in its operation, and extremely rich in its content. And it receives varied emphasis in different parts of the New Testament.

In the Synoptic Gospels, faith has the sense of accepting the truthfulness or the authenticity of someone or something. Thus "the gospel of Jesus Christ" is usually taken to mean "the gospel *about* Jesus Christ." It focuses on the person at the center of the story, on his truthfulness and authenticity. So Mark's Gospel, for example, has a great deal to say about who Jesus was, Son of God, Son of man who reliably brings the gospel of God to his people. Faith in the authenticity and truthfulness of Jesus is related to miracles, and also leads to action. It isn't the size of the faith that matters, but its reality and its obedient response to what God brings in Jesus Christ.

In the Acts of the Apostles, faith is portrayed as an instantaneous response to a challenge from God through one of his servants. It therefore has about it the character of response to evidence, usually spoken evidence, and of interpretation of events that are known to have taken place. The story of Pentecost, told by Luke in Acts 2, is a good example of faith operating in that way.

This kind of faith, however, whatever its stimulus, is understood to lead to a way of life. Those who believe are known to belong to the Way (Acts 19:23; 22:4; 24:14, 22). Faith is expected to influence the whole of their lives in a way that is recognizable and shows them to be different. In Acts there is also an emphasis upon faith as an avenue of divine power through which miracles can be performed (Acts 3:16; 14:9), an element that was present in the Synoptic Gospels too. Faith can also mean, in the Acts of the Apostles, a body of truth. Luke can refer to "the faith," meaning that which is believed (Acts 6:7; 13:8). And in a similar corporate way, being a person of faith means joining the community of the faith. People who believe are "added" and so belong (Acts 2:41-47; 16:5; 16:34; 17:4, 34).

In the writings of Paul, there are other quite distinctive understandings of faith. Some of Paul's speeches recorded in Acts prepare the way for these new perceptions. For example, faith for Paul refers to a human attitude by which we accept, helplessly, what God has done for us in Christ in order to put us in right standing with God. The Letter to the Romans is an exposition of this way of understanding faith. Faith can also mean a body of truth for Paul, as in Acts 13:38-39. But it can also mean "a believing attitude," which affects a way of life because it is central to it (Rom. 1:8; 1 Thess. 1:3, 7; 2 Thess. 1:3, 4). And Paul can also use faith in relation to a divine gift by which power can be exercised to perform miracles (1 Cor. 12:9; 13:2).

In John's Gospel, there is that sense of "believing," which means to "give credence to" something or someone (John 2:22; 4:50; 8:45). It can mean to accept intellectually. This is in common with other parts of the New Testament. In that sense John also uses faith to mean "believing that" (John 6:69; 13:19; 20:31). Particularly it can mean being convinced about certain facts. But the most significant Johannine use of "believe" really needs to be translated "believe into," or "believe on." To give credence to something, or to believe that something has happened, is the basis for committing oneself to that person and to those events. You believe yourself into them. John uses this idea of "believing into" particularly in relation to Jesus, so that expressions like "believing in his name" really mean committing oneself to Jesus as the revelation of God (John 3:16, 18; 6:29; 7:38; 10:42, 14:1).

In John also, is the very important use of believing as a form of perceiving (John 6:36; 6:46-47; 20:25-29). By faith, people see what everyone else can see, but perceive more than everyone else perceives.

This last emphasis of John enables us to look also at the Letter to the Hebrews, where faith is again multifaceted. Here, faith describes our approach to God through the way that God has opened up for us into the divine presence through Christ (Heb. 10:19-25); and it is to see through present realities to future realities that are not yet revealed (Heb. 11:1-3); and it is on the strength of those perceptions to live one's life on the basis that God is present, and that God's promises will not fail (Heb. 11:1-40).

One last element of New Testament teaching about faith that must be included here is that presented by the book of James. He is concerned to demonstrate that faith must be more than intellectual assent and that it must lead to expressions of faith in such a way that Christian activity grows out of Christian faith. The Christian deeds we perform are not, as far as James is concerned, an alternative to believing in God through Jesus Christ. They are the inalienable expression of faith, and if they are not present in someone's life, then James begs to question whether faith is present at all (James 2:16-26).

We may gather all that together in a summary offered by P. H. Menoud:

> In short the New Testament conception of belief (faith) is a confession that Jesus' declarations on his person are true, together with the apostolic witness which, after the death and resurrection of Jesus, affirmed that he is very Lord and Christ. This faith moreover implies that by it the believer is totally committed; he is bound to him who is henceforward his Lord and who makes him live in newness of life. At all times and in all places faith is at once a confession and a life renewed in obedience to Christ, who is the object of faith and confession.[2]

It is therefore important for preachers to reflect on what we mean when we use the words "faith" or "believe" in the pulpit. It is not only a matter of being clear about what precisely we mean. It also raises the question of whether our usage of words about believing are wide enough to communicate the rich content that faith has in the New Testament. Perhaps we too easily narrow it down to one or two aspects, and turn those into the whole story. If so we may be in danger of preventing people from coming to faith, whose avenue would be one of the other valid meanings. The more we limit the true meaning of faith in the New Testament, the more we are in danger of excluding people. It is like closing doors against those who want to get into the building by a way that is not familiar to us.

It must be already clear that faith and reason cannot be simply set out as opposing each other. So much of what has gone before in evidence from the New Testament requires the operation of the human mind and of reason, if in no greater task than understanding the words and ideas presented to us. The question is by what process faith and reason can be seen to relate well to each other in Christian experience.

Theology helps us here because of the very nature of theology itself. I remember as a young student reading that the difference between biblical study and theology was rather like the difference between studying plants by walking through the forest or by going to a botanical garden.[3] In the forest all the flowers and plants are undoubtedly there, but you come across them randomly, and you have to travel a very long way in order to see them all. There is also considerable repetition. In a botanical garden, however, all the various flowers and plants have been gathered together in proper relationships; they are named and identified; and if you plan the trip carefully you can see everything that there is to be seen.

Theology has been defined, quite simply, as "the science of God." I find myself more at ease with E. L. Maskell's extension of this definition as "the study of God and of God's creatures in relation to him," so long as that order is preserved. It has to be put that way, because the way we understand ourselves and the life around us is derived from and dependent upon the being of God. That being is expressed in love and grace, and God constantly seeks relationships of love and grace with all who can respond in such relationships. God's initiative and our response is the basic rhythm of the divine/human relationship. Theology is therefore properly seen as the study of God and of the rhythmic ways in which all our life relates to and may be gathered up into the life of God.

It is here that faith and reason, believing and thinking are so intimately related. As we seek to gather together the materials from the biblical forest into the theological botanical garden such great issues as the Trinity, the Incarnation, the Atonement, the Resurrection, the Ascension, and the Christian hope all challenge our faith to the depths, and our use of reason to its heights. This is not about turning Christian faith into "classroom religion." It is not to give the impression that God can somehow be captured, controlled, and described with absolute accuracy. But it is to find, through the great theological doctrines, ways in which, however partially, we may grasp the greatness of God and the wonder of God's relationship to all that he has made. Without faith, the doctrines have no reality. Without reason, they make no sense.

It is the interrelation of the two, faith and reason, which will enable our sermons to be weighty without being drab and academic; inspiring without being shrill and shallow. People who listen to our preaching, and who seek to respond to it, should have both a sense of the mysterious depth and also a sense of the energizing power of believing. There is a kind of preacher whose theological weight is such that you are constantly told about the wonderful banquet, but never invited to the table nor told how to get there. There is another kind that constantly and urgently invites you to the table and tells you how to come, without giving you any sense that what is on the table is worth the journey! Our hearers need a theological content that whets their appetite, and a faith content that enables them to enter into all that God can be in their lives.

There is a third element in the equipment of the preacher to handle faith and reason: it is the area of Christian tradition. In many ways this is a more awesome part of the journey than any other, not least because of its extent.

From the very beginning the Christians naturally engaged in theological reflection. The great councils of the church in the first five centuries struggled with the big questions that were raised, not least by new cultures into which the faith traveled. Sometimes it means that we have great difficulty with the words used, as with the identification of the Trinity in terms of "persons."

> To say that God is somehow both three and one at the same time can easily look like a highly incomprehensible kind of metaphysical mathematics, which is entirely remote from the biblical gospel, or our own living relationship with God, and our life in this world.[4]

Sometimes there is the even harder task of trying to understand the culture from which we receive some of the ideas that are part of that tradition. Theories of the Atonement are a good example here. Yet the benefits are enormous. Think of the Augustinian-Lutheran-Barthian perceptions on justification by grace through faith! Or the way John Wesley used prevenient grace to untie the knot with the sovereign God at one end and human beings with the capacity to choose at the other. Above all, entering into these theological traditions is an act of fellowship as we seek to understand what those in former days understood to be the problems, as well as trying to grasp their solutions. They still have to be received by us today through interpretation in terms of the setting in which we find ourselves. At times language, thought forms, and context are all against our being able to receive and use what is handed down. Yet continuity is often more important than relevance. The preacher who bypasses this part of the theological task is robbing himself or herself of the necessary engagement with the whole church of God in Jesus Christ, and in the process is in danger of communicating shallow perceptions to the congregations.

This is the story of the way in which the church sought, from generation to generation, not only to take her believing and her thinking seriously, but also to find the right balance in her total perception of God. In age after age one or other of the great Christian doctrines has been either greatly neglected or grossly overemphasized. Both the neglect and the overemphasis are forms of heresy. In the past we have often been hindered by limiting our perception of church tradition to that of our own denomination. There has always been plenty to get on with there! In the ecumenical era, the riches of all the churches are now available to us. The more we understand of our great traditions of theological reflection, the wiser we shall be in handling the dangers of neglect or overemphasis in our own generation, and not least in our own preaching. The adage that whoever "chooses to neglect the history of the church is condemned to live through it all again" applies as surely to our Christian traditions of doctrine as it does to any other part of the life of the Christian church.

This means more than quoting chunks from books on the history of theology, however, just as we would be wrong to pack our sermons with retellings of the various testimonies of people who have believed. What is required is that our theological learning and our faith experience should be so truly part of ourself, that what people hear in our preaching is a true fusion of reason and faith within the mind and heart of the preacher.

> It is Christ's living presence that unites a diverse tradition, yet the single center is experience in richly different ways. Christ's presence is experienced sacramentally by the liturgical traditions, ecstatically by the charismatic tradition, morally

inspiring by the liberal traditions, as ground of social experiment by the pietistic traditions, as doctrinal teacher by the scholastic traditions, as sanctifying power of persons and society by the Greek Orthodox tradition, a grace perfecting nature by the Roman Catholic tradition, as word of scripture by the evangelical tradition. Each of these traditions and the periods of their hegemony have experienced the living and risen Christ in spectacularly varied ways. But nothing else than the living Christ forms the center of this wide circumference.[5]

For this we need hard work from ourselves and warm and affirming fellowship from our preaching peers.

There is a fourth element in this journey of reason and faith together. It is the nature of human personality. Personality has been defined as "those relatively stable and enduring aspects of the individual that distinguish . . . from other people and at the same time form the basis of our predictions concerning . . . future behaviour." [6] Another defines a person as an "intricate and changing organism of chemical, biological, psychological, sociological, cultural, and spiritual interactions" who "chooses value according to his own interests and works towards many goals with ever new ingenuity, adaptability, and appraisal of gains and losses, all the while learning from and co-operating with other persons in social relationships."[7]

The detail of these definitions should not blind us to their common testimony to one fact about human personality. It is complex, and it must be treated seriously by all who wish to communicate. In particular there is the modern contention between genetic causes of our character and behavior, and the environmental influences on those two. It is sometimes referred to as the "nature" versus "nurture" interrelation. Our genetic origins do not allow us simply to behave according to nature. The laws of our land make that plain. But neither can our attempts to build a society ignore the effects our genes have upon us. We cannot become something totally different from the way we are made.

The relevance of all of this for thinking and believing, for faith and reason, is that the preacher has to allow for the variety of personality, experience, and motivation in the congregation. Some are undoubtedly more driven by emotion than by mind or will. Some are more rational than emotional or volitional. Some operate most strongly on a basis of their capacity to determine what to do and to do it. Yet we are supposed to preach to them all! And this very variety has played a significant part in the theological differences, the traditional forming of new denominations, and problems of ecumenical relationship. It is urgent that the preacher addresses such a variety in a meaningful way.

It is here that Paul's example will perhaps help us. Describing his own ministry he says: "It is he whom we proclaim, warning everyone and teaching everyone in all wisdom, so that we may present everyone mature in Christ" (Col. 1:28). He has a vision of gathering everyone, whatever their personality shape, to a process by which, through the proclamation of Christ, everyone may become whole, healthy, perfect. Our task is so to use reasonable faith, believing reason, that all who hear us are drawn toward perfection (after which John Wesley admonished all his followers to strive). What guidelines are there along the road for us as preachers?

One is the task of teaching. If we wish people truly to have a reasonable faith, they must have some sense of the content of that faith. A good preacher will have in every sermon that which informs, builds up, and enlightens those who listen, so that they are theologically more mature when they leave than when they entered. This need not turn the sermon into a lecture; indeed it must not. But neither will it leave the congregation without anything intellectually to hold on to when the sermon is over. Paul gave an important place to the mind, in that same Letter to the Romans in which he described faith so significantly. We dare not fail to teach.

Then we have a task of making sense of things. If we truly are witnesses to "transcendence in the midst" (see the David Jenkins reference in chapter 1) picking our biblical and theological material seriously, and relating it to what is happening in the world today, then people have a right to expect sermons to make sense of what is going on from a Christian point of view. They will expect us to draw from our biblical and theological basis those perceptions, principles, values, instructions, and warnings that take hold of what is happening around them, and make sense of them in the light of eternity. After all, probably the strongest point of personal witness in our world today is that Christians see the same news on television, or hear it on the radio, or read it in the newspapers, and continue to believe. The preacher has the task of enlarging that belief, not in spite of the evidence around us, but certainly in relation to it. We do not have to explain everything in order to make sense of it. But we are obliged to show that given the basic principles of the Christian faith, it makes sense to believe and to give one's life wholly in this direction; indeed it makes more sense to do that than to do anything else.

There is third the task of apologetics. Apologetics is not about making apologies. It is about what the Letter of Peter calls "giving a reason for the hope that is within" us (1 Pet. 3:15). It is to be aware of, and to hear the reasons that people advance in our generation for not believing, and to reply to those reasons on the level at which they are offered, without being unfaithful to the gospel as we have received it. It means that being aware of those popular expressions of antifaith that are current at the time, and having the courage to answer them in the name of Christ. "There is something before this achievement of a Christian line—and that is a Christian dialogue in which a given issue can be explored and known by the thinking church." [8]

In all these ways faith and reason need each other . They are not enemies unless we seek to make them so. They are both precious gifts of God. A combination of a believing reason and a reasonable faith is crucial if our preaching is to have the depth it requires and the inspiration it needs.

6

Uniformity and Variety
God's Many-Sided Grace

How is the modern preacher to be true to "the faith that was for all entrusted once delivered to the saints" (Jude 3) and yet remain able to address the variety of needs, backgrounds, experiences, and insights represented in the congregation? The question is more serious than we preachers often allow. It may well be that we, who are so deeply committed to leading as many people as possible to faith in Christ, by our content, method, and attitude in the pulpit exclude at least as many as we gather into our midst.

At an international conference, where a large variety of languages were spoken, we were all encouraged to greet one another with the words, "I love you with the love of the Lord," each in our own language. The English form of the greeting I recognized immediately. I had no difficulty with the French either. I certainly knew when it was a German who was greeting me. I had a chance with the Ibo from Nigeria, but any other African language, or Eastern European tongue, or any other part of the world, defeated me. I had to take it on trust that the words meant, "I love you with the love of the Lord." Suppose no one there had greeted me in English, French, German, or Ibo. I would have had no way, from the exercise itself, of discerning what was being said to me. I would have had some justification in feeling excluded from the conference, since no one there was speaking my language, or evidently seemed to care to do so. What if people sitting in the pew feel the same way, if not so

70————

dramatically, about the way in which we construe and commend the gospel of Jesus Christ?

William Abraham describes John Wesley as seeking "to drag all of life, kicking and screaming, into the arena of grace." Wesley understood that somehow we have to learn increasingly to address "all of life" at the point where it is, in the language that it understands, so that we may describe and make attractive "the arena of grace." That people do not so easily understand what we say, as we imagine they do, is well illustrated by the American comedian who said that he passed one of the restaurants offering "breakfast at any time." He went in and asked for "French toast during the Renaissance period"!

There are two points of tension that make this task difficult. One is the timespan separating the culture of the first century Near East, where the gospel originated and was first preached, understood, and experienced, and the culture of the late-twentieth century where we are called now to proclaim it so that people may understand and experience it. Is it possible to be faithful to that original message, and yet intelligible to men and women today?

The second tension is between the individual and the corporate in our understanding of Christianity itself. Modern English suffers gravely from its incapacity to distinguish between second person singular and second person plural. We use the word "you" for both. Shakesperean English had "thou" and "you" the singular and plural, and that makes things much easier. As an Englishman, I long for the expression from the South of the United States, which addresses a group of people as "Y'all" (you all). This tension is important at this point, because preachers can all too easily become satisfied when different individuals appreciate what we are saying and are able to respond to it. But we must not escape from that corporate sense, which raises the question of whether "they all" were able to understand and respond. Too easily we reach out well to those who think and believe as we do and who are culturally like us. We have to face the hard question put some years ago in terms of what God will say at the end if some of us come to him without bringing the others. None of us will ever be able so to describe the Christian message that everyone present will understand all that we say all the time. But that does not excuse us from seeking to do so.

One Gospel, Many Gates

The New Testament material, which provides the basis for our preaching, is itself significant as an example of sustaining a unity, which nevertheless allowed for considerable diversity. James D. G. Dunn, in the closing summary of *Unity and Diversity in the New Testament* writes:

> I think it can justly be said that we have discovered a fairly clear and consistent unifying strand which from the first both marked out Christianity as something *distinctive* and different and provided the *integrating center* for the diverse expressions of Christianity. That unifying element was the unity between the historical Jesus and the exalted Christ.[1]

Having set out the content involved in the New Testament, however, he then goes on.

> Our study has also forced us to recognize *a marked degree of diversity* within first-century Christianity. We can no longer doubt that these are many *different expression of Christianity within the New Testament*.[2]

Whether or not we accept so stark a statement we must explore its implications for preaching. The New Testament reveals a variety of ways of understanding the content of the gospel.

In Paul's Letter to the Romans, there is a powerful expression of the gospel message in series. First the Gentiles and then the Jews are argued into a corner because of their sinfulness (Rom. 1:18–3:3). Then God is shown to save us through righteousness (being right, doing right, putting in the right), which we receive by faith. We do not earn it, it is a free gift (Rom. 3:21-24). Next Paul explores how this gift is received and experienced, leading on to the experience of life through the Spirit (Rom. 5:1–8:39). There is a momentary exploration at a tangent when consideration is given to what will happen to the Jews (Rom. 9:1–11:36), and then we return to the application of this gospel to daily life (Rom. 12:1-16). Christians over the centuries have properly seen Romans as a majestic outline of how the gospel should be understood.

A major difficulty arises if that is the only way into the Kingdom, for it isn't the way that Paul came! If the three accounts of Paul's conversion in the Acts of the Apostles are in any sense accurate, then Paul did not go through the series that he later describes in Romans (Acts 9:1-19; 21:40–22:21; 26:1-23). The experience on the Damascus road was rather that of a man who goes with all the right zeal to do all the wrong things, is met by Jesus in the vision on the Damascus road, and receives a call to radical obedience that turns him around and sends him off with all the same zeal in the opposite direction. There is no mention of sin, nor atonement, of faith, or of the fullness of the Spirit. So it is hardly likely that Paul in Romans is claiming that the conceptual order in that letter is the only process by which to come into God's kingdom. Romans has been a force in Christian history (think of Augustine, Luther, Calvin, Wesley, and Barth), and that shows how fundamental it is. But the series of experiences leading to faith, set out in the letter cannot be the only way, unless Paul simply changed his mind.

In John's Gospel we find a different style of writing as well as a different way of looking at the Christian good news. Since many readers or hearers of different parts of the New Testament had only that part to reflect on, unlike us, they would have only that understanding of the gospel contained in whichever piece of the New Testament they received. In John's Gospel it would be communicated largely through the statements of Jesus' identity: "I am. . . ." It is thus about perceiving the truth, finding the way, living the life, going through the door, being cared for by the shepherd, seeing the light, being sustained in the vine, and experiencing resurrection. These images are all immensely powerful, but they do not necessarily communicate, as the focal point, the outline of Romans. There is enough there to show a direct link, as John 3:16 makes abundantly plain, but that is not the prime emphasis.

If you turn to Paul's Letter to the Colossians, you have a different picture again. Fundamental elements are still there, but this time it is about the way in which Christ must be seen in cosmic proportions. He robs the principalities and powers of their authority. Whatever spiritual beings are said to exist, Christ is superior to them all. Indeed the universe was made for him and through him.

Turn to Hebrews and the story is different again. Now the whole gospel message is seen in terms of the law, the patriarchs, the temples, the sacrifices, the high priesthood, and some of the great characters of Jewish history. In this context, Jesus as lowly brother who was made "perfect through sufferings" (Heb. 2:10), is also seen as the one through whom God "created the worlds" (Heb. 1:2). To turn back from him is to tread his blood under foot, and not to have the opportunity to repent. The picture is dramatically different from that in Romans or John or Colossians.

The readers of the letter to the Hebrews needed a detailed knowledge of the Jewish faith, in both its history and its liturgy. Within and behind the words and thoughts of this letter can be discerned the specific issue that it was addressing. Christians who had previously been Jews seemed now to be in danger of giving up their Christian faith because of the persecution they were suffering, and were inclined to turn back to their former ways. In effect, the writer to the

Hebrews puts the simple and stark question, "Where can you go that is forward after you have known faith in Jesus Christ?"

The fundamental message at the heart of all of these different ways of understanding the gospel is the same. It is focused on Jesus Christ. It depends for its meaning on Jesus being the fulfillment of what God promised through the history of the Jews. Its content had to do with the birth, growth, ministry, death, resurrection, ascension, and the future coming of Jesus Christ. He is, in a different way from any other human being, the revelation of God that provides a complete basis for saving faith in God. On this, the different ways of understanding the faith are agreed.

Where they differ has to do with the place they start in telling the story, the analogies they use to communicate it, and the understanding on which they draw from the people whom they are addressing. Both in what is actually written, and what is left unwritten but assumed to be known, one can see how the written word engages the context and the people at the receiving end. The various ways of understanding the gospel were diverse but unified.

One Gospel, Many Preachers

The New Testament reveals divergent ways of preaching the gospel also. A classic contrast is that between Acts 17:16-34 and 1 Corinthians 2:1-5. In the former, Paul, invited to address a virtual debating society, with a tradition of ruling the city of Athens, gives a speech of which the first half is a fusion of the contemporary philosophies of Epicurianism and Stoicism. He was halfway through his address before his listeners would have known that he was any different from them. Then suddenly there is a change. He is calling them to make up their minds (a concept to which they were not partial), because God had established a day of judgment, through the man whom he had raised from the dead (presumably Jesus Christ). His message had now taken a dramatic turn and was distinctly different from what either Epicureans or Stoics believed or welcomed. They made plain their dislike by mocking him, though some said they wouldn't mind hearing him again. Some few responded positively.

Paul had undoubtedly shown how the Christian faith was different from the prevalent philosophies held by the majority of people listening to him. From our point of view, however, something is missing from his message as recorded by Luke in the Acts of the Apostles. This great opportunity to present the Christian gospel to a Gentile audience said nothing about sin (though he got as far as mentioning human ignorance), nothing about the cross, nothing about the atoning death of Jesus Christ, (which figured so highly in Romans), and nothing about the nature of saving faith. By any standards of Christian judgment, Paul's speech sounded like a rather watered-down version of the Christian gospel that he defended so vigorously (for example in 1 Cor. 15:3-11 and Gal. 1:6-9).

The contrast comes out even more starkly in what follows in the story as told by Luke in the Acts of the Apostles. In that story Paul went straight from Athens to Corinth. Later, in 1 Corinthians 2:2 he writes: "For I decided to know nothing among you except Jesus Christ, and him crucified." It is a convenient solution to say that he had such a rough time on Mars Hill that he decided to change! Many preachers know the experience! But that won't do, not least because he had very significant converts in Athens, and because that kind of change would be wholly untypical of Paul as we know him from the New Testament.

The difference must have had more to do with the distinctive varied nature and culture of Athens and Corinth as well as the different occasions for his preaching in each place. It suggests that, like Jesus in the gospel, he was determined to start where people were, address issues that they could understand, and take them only as far as they were able to go on that occasion. At the same time he was able, within those limitations, to offer enough to be the basis of saving faith. As Jesus talked to a woman at a well about water (John 4:7-26), to a man with a withered hand in a synagogue about healing (Mark 3:1-6), to a man up a tree about establishing a reasonable relationship for discussion (Luke 19:1-10), so Paul talked at Athens about judgment and resurrection, but at Corinth about the cross as God's power for salvation.

I don't take this to mean that there were "different gospels," though some would say so. Writers like James Dunn have explored the question of unity and diversity about what the gospel is, with considerable care.[3] These writers related specifically to what was presented as happenings in the ministry of Jesus. This is set out in a very shortened form in 1 Corinthians 15. The celebrated English New Testament scholar, C. H. Dodd, discerned the main strands in the early Christian message, which he called the "Primitive Kerygma," largely based on the Acts of the Apostles.[4] Galatians 1:6 defends this way of looking at the gospel, without setting it out in detail there, though the rest of the letter is a defense of it. The Letter to the Romans itself is clearly an extended version of this message.

My own reflection on all of this is that there was general agreement about what the main elements of the gospel message were, but that the starting point from within that message was different from place to place, as was the amount of content covered. The determining feature as to where to begin and how far to go was plainly not the predilection of the speaker, but the condition, experience, capacity, and cultural setting of the audience. This ties in wholly with the ministry of Jesus, who started where people were, spoke to them about the things that mattered to them, used the language that they understood, and never took them further than they could follow. It was he who said to his disciples, "I still have many things to say to you, but you cannot bear them now" (John 16:12).

It is also wholly in keeping with the Christian understanding of the Incarnation as the basis of redemption. Jesus lived among us as the only way properly to reach us in a particular culture, with a particular language, at a particular time, in a particular setting. He made clear the message of the love of God, focused on those around him, but available to all. It could be communicated to those around him only as he was communicating it. Communication to the rest of the world, to whom it was also offered, could not be precisely in the language and method that he was using in the villages of Galilee. Paul, as described in the Acts of the Apostles, is not only preaching the message of Jesus, he is using the method of Jesus. Redemption is only likely to be understood and accepted when incarnation has taken place in order to embody and declare the message in a way in which it can be understood.

One Gospel, Many Responses

There was also in the New Testament a variety of ways of responding to the gospel.[5] Both in the Gospels and in Acts, remarkably different people find their way into the kingdom of God by incredibily different routes, though all through faith in Jesus Christ. Nathanael seems extremely reluctant, hovering not even at the back of the crowd but under a fig tree at some distance. When Jesus confronts him, however, he has clearly reflected very deeply on all the issues involved, and is able to make a commitment on the spot, as John tells the story (John 1:43-51). By contrast, Nicodemus comes by night (John 3:1-15). He is puzzled by what he hears, and then goes underground until John 7 when he is saying a little to defend Jesus in the Council, but puts his head down again when he is criticized only to emerge at the end of the Gospel making a public witness by going with Joseph of Arimathea to claim the body of Jesus and provide it with a grave (John 19:38-42). If you put alongside that the woman at the well in John 4:5-30, 39-41, or the man born blind in John 9:1-41, there is a wide range of ways into the Kingdom over a spread of only four people. In Acts it is even wider.

The many-sided grace of God seems to have the capacity to meet us precisely where we are, and perhaps even to address us in the light of our experience and our insights, our needs and our perceptions; but also in terms of the kind of personality drives we possess. Some are more emotional, some more rational, some more volitional, some sheerly activist. One gains the impression that whatever it is we normally are, the Spirit of God is likely to address the gospel to us along that avenue.

It is not too daring to say that in the New Testament some people seem to become Christians on totally inadequate grounds. And people have been doing so ever since. The test was not how much they knew, or on how many cylinders their engine of faith was firing. The test was whether there was enough relationship to Jesus for there to be saving faith. The rest of the Christian life is meant to be an experience of sanctification that fills out both the story and the experience.

Part of the tragedy of our Christian life today is probably that people come into the Kingdom by one route or another, and then are inclined to join all those who have come via a similar route, and therefore who have similar perceptions about what it all means. They strengthen their conviction and their sense of well-being by standing over against all the other groups who see it differently, rather than being able to learn from one another how many-sided the grace of God is in Jesus Christ.

To suggest that there are other ways possible than that by which I came in may well be taken as a threat to me and my very being as a Christian. However objective we try to be, we can all be threatened at that level.

For many years of my life, I tended to see entry into the Christian faith rather like going through a door into a tunnel. Everyone came by that same door, and so all could be located somewhere in that tunnel. All whom I found there had started as I had started, and were traveling as I was traveling. It was a comforting and secure realization and experience. After many years, however, it dawned on me that there were others who were also in the Christian faith who plainly had not come through that door, nor were traveling down that tunnel. I found out that the entrance into the kingdom of God through faith in Jesus Christ was not in fact going through a door into a tunnel, but entering a gate into an arena. The arena had many different gates, all of them clearly marked "Through Jesus Christ." But each gate led into a different part of the arena. To my great surprise I found that the Christian life was not simply exploring with those who had come through the same entrance as myself, but exploring the arena discovering how people had come to faith in Jesus Christ by another gate, and what it meant to them to be traveling in a different part of the arena. This has not diminished my faith, nor drawn me away from those with whom I first started on the Christian journey. But it has enlarged my perception of what it's all about, and in so doing has given me a larger vision of God.

The serious point for the preacher is that without this breadth among us, we may be excluding many people from the gospel. Our particular ways of understanding and responding are satisfying to us, and to those who think as we do. But what of the many outside the Christian church who are still seeking to find a way to faith in Jesus, and who find our particular approach too limited? Any preacher who keeps records of her or his preaching may submit themselves to a very simple test. Over a long enough period of time for which you have records, make a list of how many times you have preached on the different parts of the New Testament. Examine the themes you have covered. And ask yourself whether your grasp of faith in God through Jesus Christ is anywhere near as wide as that which is contained in the New Testament itself. It can be a chastening experience. Unless we are broader, how can we "drag all of life . . . into the arena of grace"?

One Gospel, Many Applications

There is also in the New Testament a variety of applications of the gospel. In Romans 13 and Revelation 13 there are two very different attitudes towards civic authority. In Romans the implication is that because the civic authorities are given by God in order to keep order, then we should obey them. In Revelation 13 there is more than a hint that the ruling authorities are evil and should be resisted. It has often been suggested that these are two conflicting ways of reflecting the Christian gospel.

Perhaps here we are helped by seeing the difference between principle and application, as they are used in the New Testament. To take the example of meat offered to idols, and the problem that created in New Testament times, I can only observe that in the village where I live in England, we have no difficulty about meat offered to idols. Our meat has not first passed through some pagan temple where it has been used as part of the religious celebrations. For religious reasons, therefore, we have no need to scruple about buying and eating the meat. It was not so in Paul's time, where many Gentile Christians felt very uneasy about eating meat that had been through that process first. The application apparently has no relevance to us.

The principle, however, is a very different matter. For the principle at the heart of that question, as Paul makes plain in writing both to the Corinthians (1 Cor. 10:23–11:1) and to the Romans (14:1-23), was the question of how the behavior of one Christian made it difficult for another Christian to continue in the faith. This is a fundamental principle of the

Christian life. It may not be relevant to meat offered to idols in industrialized countries, but it is certainly relevant to the way in which I do my work, enter into my leisure, live within my family, and determine my priorities. Other Christians can be helped or hindered by the way I go about any of those things. For the principle remains, even if the points of application differ.

That remains a very tantalizing principle in the Christian life, which has to be applied over a wide range of issues.

The principle in Romans 13 and Revelation 13 is, I think, that God has appointed civic authorities in order that citizens should be treated properly and allowed true human freedom. The application where a government is largely fulfilling this purpose is therefore that we should be obedient citizens. Where this is not so, however, as the Revelation 13 passage suggests, the Christians may well seek the removal of such a government. I believe that distinction between principle and application would help us over a wide range of issues in terms of New Testament interpretation and their application today.

In these four areas; the understanding, preaching, accepting, and applying the gospel in the New Testament, we have a model for our unity and diversity. That is not to say that there is among us a complete unity about the details of the gospel. But it is to say that the basis of our faith is rooted in what Jesus did and had done to him and in the meaning of those things for faith in God. The question for preachers is, week by week, where to begin with that story, how much of the story to tell, and where to end. The example of the New Testament would seem to suggest that a strongly determining factor in answering these questions is the nature, context, experience, and understanding of those who will be listening. On the one side we must avoid trying to lock our present culture into a first century pattern that it cannot follow: on the other side we must avoid trimming our message to what we imagine to be acceptable in the late-twentieth century. We may not copy the political candidate's conclusion: These are my convictions and if you don't like them I can change them! We have to be both true to the original gospel and relevant to our culture.

One Gospel, Six Strands

It may help us in this task to look at the major elements of the gospel story, and at the possibilities they offer us for this process of engagement.[6] There are at least six fundamental strands in the gospel story as we have it in the New Testament. First, there is *event*. Certain things happened in the life 1. and ministry of Jesus Christ, and although scholars may to this day be arguing about what happened, and about whether some things happened, no reputable scholar denies that there was a "happenedness" about the ministry of Jesus Christ. He did live, he did say and do certain things. He is properly part of history. In that sense, one of our major tasks as preachers is probably simply to tell the story. In my early days as a broadcaster, I recall the producer commenting on a script I had just read as a preparation for recording it. "You're working too hard at it," he said, "your story is good enough in itself; just tell it!" I have often reflected on that good advice for preachers. In our Western culture there is an increasing number of people who have never heard this story. Perhaps alongside our preachers we need also a guild of storytellers, who can so tell the story with meaning that people find themselves living within the story again. There are events.

But necessarily, there are also *interpretations*. Very few of 2. the events in the New Testament pass without interpretation. The nativity stories tell of the birth of a baby. But side by side they tell of the meaning of the coming of this baby. He is to be called Jesus, because he will save his people from their sins (Matt. 1:21). Mark tells us that Jesus prophesied that he was going to die. That is a matter of happenedness. But he also tells us why. He will "give his life a ransom for many" (Mark 10:45). Our task as preachers is to follow that model. It will not be enough simply to tell the story. People need also to know the meaning of the story. How many are there, I sometimes wonder, who hear our views at Christmastime, but who have never understood that it means having Jesus born in their hearts? How many come to Easter Day, without knowing the risen Lord as Lord of their lives? How many know of Pentecost without also knowing the power of the Holy Spirit within them? People need to hear not only the event, but also the interpretation.

But in the New Testament there is also *projection*. The writers ask the question not only about what Jesus means for them, but about how far the meaning of Jesus extends. Their answer is that his meaning extends to the ends of the ages. So John, in the prologue to his Gospel, introduces us to Jesus by talking about the Word. We are well into the first chapter before we discover that he is actually talking about Jesus! He gives us first the picture of the Word, who is the secret of creation. He allows different readers to bring their own understanding of this Word, a figure of speech known to Greek and Hebrew culture, with a variety of meanings in each. John allows for all of that, and then focuses them all on the person of Jesus Christ (John 1:1-18). Matthew adds that he is not only the secret of the beginning, but also the Lord of the end (Matt. 7:21-23). Everyone will have to face him at the end of life. Paul sees him as the Lord of the middle. He is not only the one for whom all things were made, and to whom all things move. He is also the sustaining principle of everything now (Col. 1:15-17).

It will not do for us as preachers to be satisfied even with events and interpretations. People need to know the extent of the faith claims we are making. The implication of the projection of the meaning of Jesus against this universal backdrop is that there will be no subject or issue with which the gospel of Jesus Christ cannot engage. That does not mean that the way to this engagement is easy. It certainly does not mean that there will be "a text for every occasion." But it does mean that Christians, basing themselves on the ministry, life, death, resurrection, ascension, and future hope connected with Jesus, will be able to discern principles, guidelines, and perspectives on modern issues that the world desperately needs.

In the fourth place there is *testimony*. Again and again the gospel story is carried forward by someone telling what it means to them that they have met Jesus and he has changed their lives. In John chapter 1, there are a number of such occasions. In John 4, it is the woman at the well. In John 9, the man born blind tells what has happened to him. The value of the testimony is that it shows that what God was offering in Jesus is relevant to ordinary life. What might otherwise be religious theory or philosophy is shown to be an experience for everyday people. The implication of this for the preacher is not that we should always be telling our own story. But it is rather that all our sermons (and we might want to add our prayers also) need to have in them those elements of human experience that demonstrate that faith is about everyday life.

Then there is also *application*. On a number of occasions, when Jesus had done something significant in a person's life, he followed the life-changing incident with an instruction. Sometimes it was a call to come and follow him (Mark 3:13-19). On other occasions it was an instruction to go and live in a different way (John 8:11). And yet other times it was to send people back home to tell their story (Mark 5:19). There is no part of the gospel that is to be heard, understood, and received and then to leave people unchanged. Those who listen to our preaching deserve to hear more than the telling of a story with its significance, the projection of the meaning, and a witness to what difference it has made to ordinary human lives, without also hearing how it applies to their daily living.

Last, there is *invitation*. In the ministry of Jesus, people were simply drawn to him. Where he went they came (John 1:35-51).

When he moved they followed (Mark 5:21, 24, 31). When he tried to get away, they followed and found him (Mark 6:47-56). When individuals asked him more, he invited them to come and see. There is about the gospel story that which excites the curiosity of the listener. We tell the remarkable events at his birth, and people ask how this might be. We encourage them to travel on. They hear about the things he did as a teacher and a healer and they wonder how an ordinary man could do that. We point them further down the road. They learn how, totally unexpectedly, the religious authorities of the day combined with the secular authorities of the day to remove this man who seemed to be doing so much good. New hearers are amazed. We invite them to walk a little further with us. They see the Last Supper; are present in the Garden of Gethsemane; go through the trial and walk along the way to Calvary. Amazement moves to heaviness and perplexity. We tell the remarkable events three days after his death. What are they to do now? We can tell them the story again if they wish it. But their curiosity will only be fully satisfied if they step inside the circle of faith, and discover these things as not only historically the basis of their faith, but also the model for their daily living.

These six basic elements in the gospel story are building blocks for preaching. They are also good markers if we wish to plan out new sermons. And they are a good test of whether a sermon has been a gospel sermon at all. Their importance here is that they enable us to reach out into the culture of our day and establish links with what is going on around us. The preacher who takes this task seriously will find herself or himself called upon to work very hard and to think very deeply and to pray very seriously. It is not an easy task. But the sense of vocation to preach, the awareness of a deepening of one's own life, and the sheer satisfaction of making the link between gospel and culture are in themselves rewards that far outweigh the work. They have to be experienced to be understood.

7
Gospel and Life
Making It Public

In the previous chapter we looked at diversity and unity, noting that one of the main reasons why we need a variety of ways of understanding, proclaiming, responding to, and applying the Christian gospel is that there is such a varied world out there that needs to hear the message. We now turn to what that means in practice.

The fact that most of our preaching happens in buildings that are often referred to as public places of worship means that preaching is a public activity. Despite our strong emphasis on the personal, and often individual nature of Christianity, we still look upon faith as public faith, both because we have to live it out in public, and because we believe it has an application to public life. In this chapter, we ask what are the implications for the preacher of being engaged in a public debate, and of expounding a public faith, simply by reason of preaching in a public place. John Habgood devotes considerable attention to the idea of Christianity as public faith, and offers a very interesting perception on how we need to go about our work. Using the Latin word *religio*, he points out that it is capable of two meanings. The first has to do with binding together. John Habgood points out that in relation to much public life, the church, or its representatives in particular places, has a certain capacity to stand apart from conflict, disputes, and confrontations. In the workplace, in business life, concerning matters of health, education, social care, and economics, the church is rarely the driving force or the controlling power. But it is able to provide a neutral space, a safe area, a broader perspective, within which parties engaged in confrontation can meet, where masks may be laid aside, and where free from the pressures of endless lobbying there is a chance of finding a solution.[1]

On the other side, Habgood points out the word *religio* also comes from a root that has to do with cutting. In that sense it is about making sharp distinctions, distinguishing between good and evil, going deeply into issues looking for truth, and therefore sometimes having to speak the words that no one wishes to hear. The church, in its responsibility as public faith, ought to fulfil that duty to the nation also. It is the prophetic, "Thou art the man," of Nathan to King David. Our question here is therefore how preaching contributes to this twofold task of binding and cutting in relation to the public issues of the day.

A second insight that must precede the detail of the chapter is provided by Lesslie Newbigin. His concern is not so much about faith as about knowledge. He notes how much of public knowledge in the Western world is dominated by the question "How?" Making the "how" approach central fits well with our modern scientific and technological age. If you can demonstrate it to be the case, then you know it. You are on firm ground when you talk about how things work. If one refers to whole areas where we do not know how things work, then the reply is that it is only a matter of time. Christians who play the "God of the gaps" game are rapidly running out of space! Our bookshops (including our Christian bookshops) are full of "how to" books.

But, says Newbigin, this is to limit our understanding of human life, and to limit the human being in a disastrous way.[2] Public knowledge ought also to be about the question "Why?" Tragically for our society, he says, the "why" questions have been relegated to the sphere of private opinion. We all accept as public knowledge the business of how things are done. When we turn to the question of why they are, it becomes a matter of private opinion. People resort to responses such as, "It may be true for you, but it need not be true for me." To change the imagery, Newbigin is saying that the "how" questions dominate the stage of public knowledge. The "why" questions are left in the wings. Until the "why" questions also become matters of public knowledge, with accepted disciplines and ways of determining answers, our culture will continue to be immeasurably limited in its perspective and our lives tragically handicapped by a restricted vision. It is the task of the Christian church to put the "why" questions back on center stage. It is not that "how" question are to be dismissed: they remain crucial. But without the element of *purpose*, the answer will remain inadequate.

There can rarely have been a better time for us to make this contribution. As we approach the end of the millennium, and the beginning of the twenty-first century, the world at large will increasingly ask questions about its past, its present, and its future. The Christian church should be a vital part of this discussion. But it is also true that in so many areas of knowledge there is taking place a gathering process whereby individual pieces of research are being brought together, conclusions are being reached, and new questions are being posed that are about nothing less than the future of humankind itself.[3]

Paul Kennedy reminds us of the 1998 anniversary of Malthus's writing nearly two hundred years ago and his gloomy prognostications about the future of the world.[4] Malthus said that there would be not enough food for our population, though as Kennedy points out he could not have known about the coming agrarian and industrial revolutions, nor about the possibilities of emigration. But Kennedy presents us with a fairly gloomy parallel picture nonetheless. The overpopulating world is still overpopulating, the underpopulating world is still underpopulating. The underpopulating world solves its problems by increased mechanization and computerization, which reduces the need for large numbers of people to work, which is the worst possible news the overpopulating world could receive. The establishing of boundaries around nations more firmly, rather than less firmly, makes movement from the poorer parts of the world to the richer parts more and more difficult. We might add now the breakdown of the confrontational attitude between the USSR and the USA, which for all its threat provided us with a certain amount of stability for forty to fifty years. At least we all knew where we were. It has been replaced by the rush into new power bloc; hence the furious debates in Britain about entry into Europe, the growing sense of power in Southeast Asia, the growing possibilities in Africa and the South Pacific, often spoiled by racism of a most vicious kind, supported by geography, politics, language, and sadly, religion.

When Kennedy asks whether there is energy and desire among the richer nations of the world to make it possible for the poorer to have what they need, he plainly does not hold out much hope. Is that not a question to which the Christian church should be seeking to offer an answer? We follow a Master who seemed to be with the poor by habit and with the rich by invitation. For us to preach Sunday by Sunday as though these things were not taking place is rather like the rich man Dives enjoying his food while Lazarus dies at his door suffering from suppurating wounds. In that setting, churches become a shelter from the realities of life around the world, rather than a launching pad from which to engage ourselves with these very problems. If we believe what Jesus said about the poor, there is no way in which our preaching can neglect the poor.

Another aspect of the problem is raised by Francis Fukuyama. He asks about the survival of humankind in the light of the development of our modern liberal society. If we have found, in liberal democracy, the best way of relating to one another, is there not a danger that we are at the end of genuine challenges that cause us to grow and develop? If so, what is the future of humankind?

In the course of that argument, Fukuyama raises the question of legitimacy.[5] He argues that a particular form of government, whatever form it be, can only survive while the people of that nation, in their social and cultural context, are willing to accept that that is a legitimate form of government. The question of legitimacy is one that we face also as Christians. On what grounds do we claim the authority of a first century wandering preacher in relation to our high-tech, internet-dominated society? How can the teacher from the shores of Galilee have anything to say to Bosnia, Northern Ireland, the Middle East, and South Africa? How do we establish our legitimacy, in order to offer our comment, as public preachers of public faith in public places?

From another perspective altogether, Steve Jones offers a similar challenge.[6] As a geneticist, he traces the early movements of our populations, and works out the implications of the world gene bank at present being compiled. In particular he focuses attention on the limitations, as well as the possibilities, of knowing so much about our own genetic fingerprints. Because we know more and more about our *nature*, we become more and more responsible for our *nurture*. What is our understanding of this nature/nurture axis? How does it relate to our understanding of human sinfulness, the offer of salvation, and the possibility of holiness? If the preacher cannot help people to discern the joining points for such a discussion, where will they learn them?

Then there are the specifically medical questions now being raised at this crucial moment in time. Although not writing in the medical field, Lesslie Newbigin foreshadowed the present situation in his book, *The Other Side of 1984*. There he argued that the age of Enlightenment is drawing to a close and its weaknesses are being more and more clearly revealed. I would want to express this by putting it in another way. The possibilities now being made available to us by medical science are either the greatest opportunities for freedom that human beings have ever had, or they are the greatest threats to life that we have ever faced. Soon, if you spit into a test tube a doctor will be able to tell you from which diseases you are likely to die, and from which you are likely to be free, and when. Do we want that information? If we don't, then there may be others that do. What about the insurers, for example? Or those who might employ us? Or even a prospective life's partner? The question of whether or not we want these things can't be avoided. The answers we give are heavy with implication for the future of humankind. How would this public faith engage with such public issues?

We ask ourselves whether we as Christian preachers have any familiar ground over which to travel in dealing with questions of this kind. I believe we have. It would be good to look at that ground before we ask ourselves about specific theological material that is at our disposal for this conversation in public faith. Where may we stand to face these issues?

Our corporate and community sense within the Christian faith has always been fundamental, and not just in terms of our Old Testament origins. Abram, Moses, and Joshua are more than simply leaders of a people. Jacob equals Israel and the corporate sense predominates in much of the Old Testament. The individual element is of course strongly present, too, and Abram, Moses, Joshua, Isaiah, Jeremiah, and Amos are all personally and individually answerable to God. Ezekiel makes that message abundantly plain. In the New Testament equally, the figures of John the Baptist and Paul as individuals, are totally necessary for the outworking of the story. But the corporate setting is powerfully there too. The place of the community of believers as the Body of Christ is indispensable (1 Cor. 12:12-31). The fact that in Christ there is neither Jew nor Gentile, male nor female, slave nor free, is another element in the story (Gal. 3:27-28). So is Paul's lovely affirmation in Romans 12:5, that each of us belongs to all the others. The picture of Christ the cosmic Lord, as it emerges particularly in Colossians, carries even wider connotations (Col. 1:15-23). The materials are already there in our scriptures and in our tradition.

Our individual salvation concepts are susceptible of corporate interpretation also. It is not simply that sheep and goats representing the nations form part of a story by Jesus, nor that Paul talks about the whole creation groaning and travailing together until now, in Romans 8:22. It is that many of our individual salvation concepts are capable of corporate application. When I watched bits of the Berlin Wall being pulled out, and people marching through from east to west, I started to sing "My chains fell off, my heart was free, I rose went forth and followed thee."[7] Now I know the words don't match the events I was watching, but the mood and the spirit was the same. Corporate sin is not so difficult to describe. Corporate salvation is something that tantalizingly invites us to further exploration.

It has always been fundamental for us to be wanting primarily to answer the "why" questions, rather than simply the "how" questions. For individual, community, and cosmic realities, we need to put the "why" question at the center of our concern. Even if we are dealing with contentious matters such as the creation stories in Genesis, or theories of the Atonement, we have learned that the "why" questions are more important than the "how" questions. To battle purely at the level of the "how" is to neglect our major contribution in relation to the meaning of the universe.

Another part of our armory for this battle is that the Christian church has regularly and frequently had to pass through dramatic changes of context since our first century beginnings. One thinks of the admission of the Gentiles into the largely Jewish Christian church, recorded by Luke in Acts 15. There was the conversion of the Emperor Constantine, before which Christians had tended often to be persecuted within the Roman Empire, but after which it became a popular thing to be. There was the East/West struggle across the first millennium between Pope and Emperor, introducing all kinds of (some unwelcome) elements in the understanding of Christianity. Then came the Renaissance, with the shift to understanding God more through human models and to questions of shape and language and movement and detail, and to the elevating of philosophy alongside theology rather than as part of it. The Reformation, which followed, was a great spiritual explosion, perhaps not primarily about doctrine but primarily about the possibility of an individual experience of God, and of all Christians being able to read and understand the Scriptures for themselves. There was freedom of faith, irrespective of what one's king or prince believed. With it came the potential of freedom from faith altogether and certainly freedom to separate from other believers with whom one disagreed, with all the possibilities of sectarianism that followed. Seventeenth-century Britain witnessed the civil wars, with strong religious content and motivation. The eighteenth century saw the evangelical revival, and then bit by bit the Enlightenment, the Renaissance, and the Reformation prepared the way for the scientific and technological revolutions of the nineteenth and twentieth centuries.

Each one of these was an enormous change for the context, and for the experience of Christians. The organized church was put under the most enormous pressures and changes—some subtle, some less so—had to take place. In each age people despaired of the future of the Christian faith. Yet the beautiful Book of Kells with its illustrated Gospels, was being prepared at a time when people were forecasting the end of Christianity. Voltaire prophesied that the Bible would be a forgotten book by the time his works had gone once around the world; a prophecy written in a house that one day was to become a distributing center for the British and Foreign Bible Society! Karl Marx saw religion steadily dying in face of the revolution that he initiated. All have come and gone; and yet still the church survives. We are not without experience of change.

Moreover it is in our tradition that we are a death and resurrection people. The heart of our faith, symbolized in our sacraments, and contained in our preaching, is that we are those who not only believe that Jesus died and rose again, but who also seek to experience dying and rising daily as the motif of our lives. We are fundamentally a pilgrim people, constantly admonishing one another against carrying too much baggage for the journey. It is not the best part of our tradition simply to resist all change for the sake of it. It is that change that is basic to our ethos as Christians.

Given then that we are able to perceive some of the major forces that are changing the world and the directions in which they are moving us; and given that we have in our tradition as Christians adequate experience of responding to changes, however painful; the question still remains whether we are theologically endowed to reach judgments on these matters in our age, and to guide our people through our preaching about which of the proposed new avenues we perceive to be provided by God.

We have our doctrine of creation. This is not to take us back to the whole question, but rather to deal with the "why" and its consequences. What are the implications, for example, of our being made in the image of God? It is at very least to have the capacity to stand apart from what goes on around us, to observe it, reach conclusions about it, live according to those conclusions, and take the consequences. It is to be not only stewards of God's creation, but also to be cocreators with God. In that light we can rightly ask how far modern experiences of cocreation are in accordance with the being of God . But our Creation theology is also about human beings having a responsibility for one another, so that none can be wholly happy until all are happy. It is about learning that nothing we have is ours by right, but all through the gracious giving of God, to whom it must one day be returned. And it is to see that we find contentment only as we seek the well-being of others and of our total environment. There are significant results when these theological perceptions are brought into dialogue with modern scientific, economic, and political thought.

Then we have our doctrine of the Incarnation. God does not simply send us messages at a distance but has come alongside us in Jesus Christ in whose life and teaching, dying, rising and ascending, there is not simply a set of incidents to be studied or learned from but a pattern of life to be lived. Paul's parabola of Jesus, from glory to glory via death and resurrection, set out in Philippians 2, is a single rhythmic movement of the love of God for humanity. Its telling is like a seamless garment. Or there is Paul's beautiful account of the ministry of Jesus, and particularly his dying, in his Second Letter to the Corinthians; "You know the generous act of our Lord Jesus Christ, that though he was rich, yet for your sakes he became poor, so that by his poverty you might become rich" (8:9). What happens to our modern debate when the concept of lowly, suffering, vulnerable love on behalf of the needy is inserted? And what might happen if this were perceived to be the strongest force in the world?

Then central to all that we believe as Christians is the idea of Redemption. No discussion on political and social relationships can be the same once the possibility of repentance, conversion, new beginnings, and change is introduced from the Christian point of view. I remember how one of the leading English authorities on South Africa, who had himself lived in South Africa many years, replied when asked how he felt about the signs of the crumbling edifice of apartheid. Very gently he replied, "I haven't yet heard the word *repentance*." Wonderfully, that word was to come, and that element to be expressed, at least by enough people for the new sharing of life in South Africa to take place. Once repentance and forgiveness and new beginnings are allowed, the most unusual things take place.

The formulation of our belief in terms of the Trinity is also highly relevant here as Colin Dunton has shown.[8] There is an idea of community. It is a community of love, where each is willing to do what needs to be done for the good of others, irrespective of status or rights. Graciousness outruns all other attitudes where the divine trinitarian model is at the center of human behavior. The "how" question about the mathematics and physics of three in one and one in three is replaced by a much more serious perception that a trinitarian theology is about how life ought to be.

Nor may we neglect the place of the Holy Spirit in this theological discussion. A picture of the Holy Spirit based on the whole of the Bible is much more far-reaching than that which narrowly locates the Spirit's activity in the individual lives of believers. It is no coincidence that so many of the elements of the Pentecost account in Acts 2 pick up the ideas of the powerful creation activities of Genesis. The Spirit of God that brooded over the former's chaos and brought order is the same Spirit of God who descends on the new creation of God on the Day of Pentecost. The giftedness of the church of Jesus Christ, about which Paul writes on a number of occasions, is a sign of the giftedness of all creation through God's grace by his Spirit. The fruit of the Spirit, about which again Paul writes in order to help the Christian church to enter fully into its heritage, points to those qualities around which the whole of life is meant to revolve. The Holy Spirit who inspires the preacher and the prophet, the evangelist and the teacher, is also the one who inspires the musician and the poet, the artist and the philosopher. Our calling as preachers is, from the platform of our experience of the Spirit's gifts and fruit, to call the world to recognize the presence of the Spirit in its midst also, as the source of everything that is lovely and beautiful and true. We seek to help others to recognize the Spirit of God in their lives already via those experiences, in order that they may perceive the more deep possibilities of the gifts and the fruit that are given to God's people through Jesus.

Our theological content also requires us to speak of judgment. God's gift to creation is a moral world. We do reap what we sow, both here and in eternity. All judgments are not relative. We will all surely answer for the way we behave. Right and wrong are meaningful categories, however complicated the definitions may sometimes be in our complex modern life. There will be a calling to account. History is linear and not cyclical, and that line will eventually bring us to God's judgment seat in Christ. Our contribution to public life, through public faith, requires us at times to condemn, and to warn, though with tears in our eyes.

Yousuf Karsh is acknowledged to be the world's greatest portrait photographer. It was said of him that his work, "sets each study apart as an individual discovery."[9] The great, the good, and the ordinary have their separate personalities revealed by his superb artistry. On one occasion, however, his portrait is of a person's back. The main part of the photograph is the wall of a French abbey. The subject of the portrait is a man sitting on an upright chair, playing an instrument. The head is bald, apart from a tonsure of hair around the ears. When asked why he did this portrait, it is said that Karsh replied that it reminded him of the loneliness of the Exile and of the loneliness that comes from being at the top of one's profession. The subject of the portrait is actually Pablo Cassals, the world famous cellist. It is reported that on one occasion this portrait, alongside many others, was put on display in a gallery. One old man came each day and stood before the Pablo Cassals portrait, taking no notice of any other. After a week of this behavior, the supervisor felt that some questions were required. He approached the old man as he stood before the portrait, and quietly asked him why he came each day, stayed so long, and stood only before this portrait. The response he got was, "Shh, can't you tell I'm listening to the music?" Our preaching as a matter of public faith may not best be expressed by using the pulpit to commend new schemes of politics or economics, of health or education. Nor may it best be done through strident criticisms of those who are in authority. It may be rather to play the music of the gospel with all its implications for life in the world. We explore the heights and depths of gospel harmony for the benefit of those who must live in the market square.

8

Evangelistic Content
Dimension and Intention

Preachers often wonder what people in the congregation think is the preacher's main task. At times we are tempted to carry out a poll to discover the answer to that question. Perhaps we preachers would rather not know! William Lutz describes the capacity in the United States for what he calls "double-speak."[1] He gives examples of how industrialists use it in order to describe giving people the sack. They talk about "head count adjustment," or "negative employee retention." A big oil company getting rid of 500 people said it was "downsizing our personnel." As a spokesman said, "We are managing our staff resources. Sometimes you manage them up and sometimes you manage them down." Mobil Oil announced that it had, "surplused" twenty-seven mechanics, and the giant telephone company A. T. & T. announced a "forced management plan to correct force imbalances." Not to be outdone, General Motors announced, "General Motors Corporation today reported a volume related production schedule adjustment at its Framing-ham Assembly Plant." This meant that it was shutting down the factory. Chrysler, a rival of General Motors, laid off 5,000 workers at Kenosha, Wisconsin, and said that it was, "initiating a career alternative enhancement program."

Now it may be that each of the individuals responsible for those various examples was seeking to soften the blow as much as possible. After all, giving people the sack is not an easy thing to do. Our propensity to obscure the message, however, is overwhelming. It amounts to a corporate disguising of the reality of what is happening.

Our task as preachers is to be as clear as possible as we follow the example of our Lord Jesus Christ, who called people to enter the kingdom of God. That involves, as Jesus himself made plain, repentance and faith. It is not so much a matter of being forced to do something, or of being overtaken by something. It rather has to do with a recognition of something about oneself, and something about God, and with positively opting to belong to God's kingdom. Peter, on the Day of Pentecost, puts it slightly differently when he assures all who listen to him that "everyone who calls on the name of the Lord shall be saved" (Acts 2:21). Paul puts it even more sharply when he says to the people in Corinth, "Be reconciled to God" (2 Cor. 5:20).

One must add at once, of course, that the preacher is about more than calling people to enter the Kingdom. We are charged also to build up in the faith those who hear us. Our aim, if we follow Paul's advice, is to seek to "present everyone mature in Christ" (Col. 1:28). But even that challenge to maturity is made within the context of a conscious commitment to the kingdom of God, a deliberate calling upon the name of the Lord to be saved, and a determination to remain reconciled to God. There is not one gospel for the unconverted, and another for the converted. We all stand under its judgment, and we all need its grace, and we all are invited to avail ourselves of that grace by the commitment of ourselves, always. Conversion is not the end of the climb: it is the beginning.

So I return to my question: Do most people who listen to us, not to mention to those who rarely listen to us, realize that this is what we are about? If they don't realize this, could it be that we haven't told them clearly enough? Are we, however innocently, guilty of "doublespeak"? I love the cartoon that shows the first-century Jew holding a sick child for the disciple of Jesus to do something about it. The disciple is saying, "As Jesus says, some kinds only come out as we create psychological conditions that optimize the natural tendency of the nervous system to stabilize itself." We may not have descended as far into healing jargon as that, but there are no prizes for being as near to it as possible.

Bishop Lesslie Newbigin has offered an important distinction for our consideration at this point. He draws attention to the difference between missionary *dimension* and missionary *intention*. Most activities of a Christian church does have a missionary dimension to them. Even the building of a church declares that the Christian faith is alive. It points to the existence of God inviting others to join us in making the journey if they so wish. If we hold a Sunday school, organize a social activity, or train a choir, the missionary dimension is present, because it is all part of our way of serving God, and it is an invitation to others to join us. Bishop Newbigin's point is that we have tended to be satisfied with the missionary *dimension*. We have neglected the missionary *intention*.

That intention comes from the instructions of Jesus himself to his disciples to go into all the world and preach the gospel. That is not a matter of dimension only. Paul's missionary journeys were dominated by missionary intention. He went to the major cities of the Roman world, and in each place tried to find the most significant situation in which to preach the gospel. He called people to turn to God through Jesus Christ and become part of the Body of Christ. Bishop Newbigin's question is whether we have followed that intention as we ought. My guess is that our failure to do so is one of the reasons why the Christian church in the Western world is not growing. But how are preachers to play their part in remedying this situation?

Speaking in Parables

The evangelistic method of Jesus will perhaps show us the way forward. His use of parables is at the forefront of this method. There is much to be said for Matthew Henry's description of parable as "a shell that holds good fruit *for* the diligent, but keeps it *from* the slothful."[2] That is, the parable method does not force the gospel on people. It provides a way by which those who are in earnest can come for the truth. It does not make the gospel crystal clear without response, since the good news from God is about a relationship, and a relationship requires some kind of willingness on each side.

The parable of the sower is probably the best example of this element of Jesus' teaching about evangelism. If, as has long been held, each parable has one particular meaning only, then it is clear that the meaning of this parable is not about the failure of some to respond. As A. M. Hunter pointed out many years ago, a return of thirty or sixty or one hundred percent would be absolutely remarkable![3] A return of ten percent was considered a good yield by the farmers whom Jesus was describing. The secret cannot lie there.

The clue to the meaning of the parable lies in the one variable factor in the whole story. The seed, the sower, the climate, and the environment were all invariable. There is no criticism of the quality of the seed. The sower is not blamed for his skill in sowing. The climate and the environment are just as they were all the year round. The one variable fact is the variety of types of soil.

Jesus seems to be saying that no matter how good the seed or how skilled the sower, nor even how predictable the climate and the setting, if the quality of the soil is not good then the harvest will be reduced.

For the preacher, this has startling significance. It suggests that however good the sermon, and however well delivered, in whatever kind of congenial setting, if the mental, moral, and spiritual state of the hearers is not right then there will be no lasting response. It is like shouting advice on the best schemes for home decoration to a set of color-blind people. However glad we are to have fulfilled our function, and however favorably they seem to have received our contribution, the advice we have given will be useless.

In this connection, we may observe that the church has been best at seed preservation; quite good at seed distribution; but rather bad at soil preparation. We may also have made a mistake in regarding the preparation of people's lives to receive the gospel as "pre-evangelism." What the parable of the sower seems to suggest is that the preparation of the soil is also part of the sower's task if there is to be a full harvest. The preparation of hearts and minds to be in a state to receive the good news of Jesus Christ is a proper part of the preacher's task. It is the task of every preacher who wishes to take the evangelistic content of preaching seriously. As R. A. Cole has observed, "The hard heart, the shallow heart, the overcrowded heart and the good heart, all are in fact present, wherever the Word of God is preached."[4] The question raised here is how we are to encourage the good heart; how do we deal with the hard heart; and how do we reach the shallow and the overcrowded hearts so that they may be able to accept the gospel.

Hendrik Kraemer helps us forward with the distinction between *communication of* and *communication between*. Communication of the content of the gospel message is fundamental to the preacher's task. What Kraemer is asking there is adequate *communication between*, in this case the preacher and the congregation, for people to be helped to receive what is being communicated. Communication between "involves the communicator having somehow discerned which are the obstacles to the receipt of the message, in such a way as to be able to meet the listener on her or his own ground."[5]

It is easy, and by no means inaccurate, to trace the hardness, the shallowness, and the overcrowdedness of men and women's hearts back to human sinfulness. We know that to be the source of all that hinders the well-being of the gospel in the world. But there are symptoms of that universal disease that can be dealt with. And they occur in circumstances with which we are all familiar. Part of the preacher's assault on the sinfulness of human nature involves addressing those symptoms, and dealing with those circumstances. This is what the preparation of the soil is about.

There are questions about the very existence of God, in the light of a still popular view that science somehow has removed the need for God. There is the prevalence of materialism in our culture, an attitude that suggests that the material world is all that we have, and that the supernatural has no place in modern life. There is a dismissal of any idea of an afterlife, on the basis of the rather cynical view that this life is all we've got. At the very level of the purpose of life, there is a humanism that suggests that human beings must be, and are capable of being, as good to one another as possible. There is also an attitude to knowledge that everything is relative and therefore there are no absolutes and no ultimate values. And there is a sense of hopelessness, felt by many in our culture, as they know more and more about what is going on around the world, and yet feel less and less able to do anything about it.

Whenever the preacher is addressing these issues in an intelligible way for the sake of the gospel, then the *communication between* is going on, and the soil is being prepared. This requires from the preacher an awareness of modern issues, and a willingness to address them in the light of the gospel. It is part of the evangelistic task.

There is a second element in the evangelistic task of the preacher that emerges from another parable of Jesus. In the parable of the secret growth, the point is that the farmer can till the ground, and put in the seed, but unless there is a power of growth that operates independently of what he does, there will be no harvest (Mark 4:26-29). In the same way the preacher as evangelist must recognize that there is a power at work in the gospel message itself, a power that the preacher neither initiates nor controls. As Paul puts it to the Romans, "The gospel is the power of God for salvation to everyone who has faith" (Rom. 1:16). A. M. Hunter observes that the gospel is about, "unremarkable beginnings, unimaginable endings."[6] When the soil has been tilled, the message proclaimed, there is a power of God at work.

There is a third shaft of light from the parables about the evangelistic task of preaching. The parable of the mustard seed suggests that not only is there a power at work to create a response to the gospel message, but also that the response will be out of all proportion to what is expected. The mustard seed becomes a huge tree. As Professor Morna Hooker put it:

> But what the kingdom will finally be is a very different matter: its greatness comes by the power of God, as silent and mysterious and inevitable as the power of growth.[7]

Given that there is a task of tilling to perform, and that there is a hidden power at work within the gospel, which will produce far more than we can expect, are there guidelines that a preacher may set for the overall task of evangelism at the heart of the proclaimed message?

A World-Changing Event

We can help people to know that the gospel is good news for them. The word translated *gospel*, is the Greek word *euangelion*, and did not originally mean a *story* as a *written document*. Its original meaning was "an epoch making event." The birth of the Emperor Augustus was described as *euangelion*.

The use of the word *gospel* or *good news*, is therefore meant to describe the fact that in Jesus Christ, God has done something for the world that is an epoch-making event and that offers salvation for everyone. The invitation of the gospel is that we might enter into the meaning of that epoch-making event. The salvation that is offered in Jesus Christ is meant to be taken up by us individually. It is as Cardinal Hume put it, "when God moves from being a Sunday acquaintance to being a weekday friend." We are called to encourage people to enter into that story for themselves.

Then there is also the task of helping people to understand good news more widely. If, as has already been suggested,

Jesus is the Word of Creation as well as the Word of Redemption, then the good news that he embodies can relate to every area of life. As part of the evangelistic task, we are meant to show how this good news relates to economics and politics, to social welfare, education, wealth, race and class, and international activity. There is no part of life to which it does not have relevance. People have a right to expect the preacher to show that to be the case.

This means in the third place that we need to demonstrate that the good news in Jesus Christ has practical implications. Our sermons need to show that God's love for us in Christ finds physical expression in the world. During a visit to Rome my wife and I were invited to join the Community of St. Egidio. It is a Roman Catholic community, consisting almost entirely of young people. They meet each evening in their chapel for a service of preaching and prayer. During the week they run a cafe for refugees and street people. They have a home for children, some of whom are HIV positive. As a community they were taught to read the Bible by, of all people, a Waldensian professor. They see the gospel in quite simple terms. It is good news for the salvation that Jesus brought through his life and death and resurrection. It therefore means that we become the embodiment of that love to the world, and for them that means reaching to the lowliest, the poorest, and the neediest. For two Protestants like my wife and myself, it was a most moving experience to see Roman Catholic sisters and brothers living out the practical implications of the gospel.

In the fourth place, our preaching task involves enabling our hearers themselves to articulate the good news. In that sense we are not only teachers, but also models. By the way in which we tell the story, interpret the events, show the implications for the world, and offer human testimony to its meaning, we are ourselves enabling those who listen to us to enter into the gospel, but also providing a model for them to make their own witness.

And we have to ensure that our preaching is a celebration of the gospel. Too much attention to method can easily give the impression that somehow we control the good news. But it came independently of us, its power is not in our possession, and we may only preach it because it has changed our lives. So our preaching must be not only an exposition and an application, but also a celebration, so that we, like those who listen to us, may join in the party. We shall never understand it wholly. There will always be more to discover. It will constantly make greater demands upon us, and provide greater satisfaction to us. That is something to celebrate again and again, and there is no better place to do so than in the context of worship when the Word of God is preached.

Personal Response

There is one last question we often ask: What is the place of the "altar call" in our modern understanding of evangelism? Is there room for this way of enabling people, who feel that they have been deeply touched by something said in a sermon, there and then to make their way forward as an act of personal dedication to Christ?

First we must notice the element of decisiveness in the biblical story. From Abram through Moses, Gideon, Jeremiah, Amos to Matthew, Peter, James, John, and Paul there is the recurring element of a call from God that requires a decisive response. God's provision for us is too great to be rejected or neglected. The issues are too large for lukewarmness. The time is too pressing for delay. "Now is the acceptable time . . . now is the day of salvation," wrote Paul in 2 Corinthians 6:2. This note is sounded even more clearly in Rom. 12:1: "I appeal to you therefore, brothers and sisters, by the mercies of God, to present your bodies. . . ." The word *appeal* is a very strong one. The basis of the appeal is what God has already done for us in Christ. The tense of the verb *to present* is aorist, meaning a decisive action complete in itself. You can almost hear, under the disciple's tones, the voice of the master who went from place to place calling people to come, take up the cross and follow, and not to wait behind seeing to business, settling affairs, or getting things straight at home. There is a holy urgency about it all, requiring a decisive response.

Even so we must ask why this has to be a public commitment, attached to a date, place, and recorded time. Let me say again that in my opinion it does not. Some will never make a public response in this way, nor should they. God deals with us as we are. Yet there is a great deal in our biblical tradition to challenge the extremely individualistic view of religion so typical of our culture. Most Old Testament moments of commitment were public, whether in sacrifice or service. The idea of individual responses unrelated to the group was an unusual one. The psalmist writes again and again about public acts of praise, dedication, and perception of God's ways. In New Testament terms there is a constant sense of the group as the context for the individual's call, response, and growth. Indeed Jesus on occasions precisely refused people's attempts at a private deal, whether with James and John over the best seats in the Kingdom (Mark 10:35-40), or with Peter over the nature of discipleship (John 21:15-23). Paul gives clear expression to this in Romans 12:5; "So we, who are many, are one body in Christ, and individually we are members one of another." In our biblical heritage, the group of the faithful is the arena of testimony, the setting for commitment, and the source of support and strength. Where better for public responses to be made?

Of course we must accept the claim that our sacraments and other great formal acts of worship already provide for public response. What more do we need than baptism once for all, Confirmation, regular Holy Communion, and annual Covenant? I would want to argue that these great sacramental and ritual acts are not exclusive of individual public commitment or renewal of the kind I am now describing.

Rather each needs the other. Exclusiveness either way narrows down the richness of our understanding and our experience. In fact each lends deeper meaning to the other. For example, the baptism of infants looks forward to the time when the child will enter into personal discipleship of Jesus Christ. For some this may happen gradually, but for others there is a significant moment of commitment. For many of that group the commitment is expressed in a public response. Those who baptize believers are careful to ensure that the baptized are truly believers.

Many of these have come via a public commitment. The same is true with our service of Confirmation. It presupposes a state of commitment. The Lord's Supper, Holy Communion, or Eucharist is for Christians a renewal of commitment. It therefore assumes prior commitment. Moreover its nature and setting do not always provide for the exposition of scripture that leads to the kind of public, intentional, particular response for which the public appeal provides. The Covenant service says it all; but crises, calls, and renewals do not wait until the first Sunday of each calendar year. These great set services provide the permanent frame of reference and understanding for any first or subsequent commitments. The commitments bring renewed meaning and depth to our participation in the great services. Sometimes both happen at once, often they do not. It is wonderful that God deals with us in the light of the fickleness and reality of human existence.

The interrelation between these two ways of looking at Christian experience becomes clear as we face another question. Do not appeals for public response lay too much stress on what we do, and not enough on what God does? Cannot they even encourage what is called pelagianism—the idea that we play a fundamental part in our own salvation? Of course that is possible. Much depends on how the appeal is made and on the preaching foundation for the appeal. But we must remember that what is being asked for is a response, not response to the appeal but a response to what God has done for us in Christ. Our sacraments make that clear by rite and symbol, so should our preaching by word and illustration. The ground for giving ourselves wholly to God is that God first gave wholly to us in Christ. By contrast with that our self-giving is responsive and noninitiatory. In any case Wesley's doctrine of prevenient grace, God's hidden activity enabling any decision for good that is made, should protect us from the errors of salvation by works.

At this point we may face another question. Does not the appeal for the open response of conversion or for subsequent responses at significant moments, lay too much stress on these particular moments over against the more settled image of growth into faith and growth in faith thereafter? Again the two are not meant to be mutually exclusive. The steady growth model is both biblically defensible and naturally congenial to some. The crisis experience and subsequent high moments of commitment are also biblically based and emotionally more suitable to others. What is more, many of us operate on a basis of both. Our wisest course is surely to be open to any way in which our discipleship may be deepened, which means that we preachers need to provide for those different ways in our conduct of worship services and meetings.

Should not this kind of first commitment and deepened commitment be happening in our fellowship and other small groups? I am sure it should and I am sure it does, but in many congregations, Methodists have no such groups where responses of this kind are expected or possible. When they do have such opportunities, maybe responses to the altar call will dry up. For the moment, however, it not only provides some with a vivifying opportunity, it also reminds all that God's grace calls for an answer. Jesus brought crisis (Greek word *krisis* is judgment) everywhere he went. Those little stories that we call parables were actually deeply disturbing challenges to the lifestyle and attitudes of the hearers. They divided the crowd into those who would respond and those who would not. This was one of the reasons why people could not ignore him.

The appeal—and therefore the hearers—can of course be abused. A preacher can manipulate an audience. Undue psychological pressure can be brought to bear. The preacher can be more interested in getting a response than in the integrity of what is being done. But where the preacher is concerned simply to enable members of the congregation to express a natural response to the grace of God, willing to risk reputation in a concern that the appeal does no more than enable that response, and where there is a desire to be in harmony with what God the Spirit is seeking to do, there can be a genuine work of grace. The testimony of those who have made responses certainly bears this out. It is for this that the preacher needs to pray and work.

I am not of course suggesting that this should be done every week. I am a privileged person in that my visits are so rare to any one place. I try to make certain that the pastor and the leaders know what I intend to do. I try to ensure that there will be those present who will be able to counsel. I do not enquire of people why they come forward. I do believe that from time to time it provides a necessary context within which the gospel is proclaimed.

Is there any particular rationale for the public appeal, either for conversion or renewal of commitment? Alongside the strands outlined above—corporateness, decisiveness, testimony and support, all based on response to what God has done in Jesus Christ—I add one further logical and psychological point. If we wish to give ourselves wholly to God there is something to be said for moving ourselves wholly, that is bodily, for God! For many people such action, of walking forward to a particular area in an act of worship, expresses, symbolizes, embodies, and even releases that deeper commitment that otherwise remains cerebral, internalized, and even trapped within our individualized world. For all these reasons I suggest that the altar call still has a necessary place among us.

9
Text and Context
It's Okay to Be Interesting

We turn to the detailed question of how an evangelical theology guides the preparation of our sermons. The great theological and biblical issues with which we have been concerned provide the necessary stimulus for our work. But they do not of themselves prepare next Sunday's sermon! The last chapter will deal with the person and preparation of the preacher as an individual. Here we concern ourselves with the question of how to get at the meaning of the text, and how to communicate that meaning, in the context of the people who come to worship. One of the main theological concerns in this book has been that the preacher should not exclude anyone from understanding and therefore responding. This concern sharpens when we look at specific preparation for a particular sermon. Two stories may make the point.

When the World Soccer Cup Finals were played in Italy, one of the highlights became the theme song, "Nessum Dorma," sung by Pavarotti. There was a totally unexpected result. Thousands of football supporters in Britain, switching on to watch the soccer, became captivated by the singer. Music shops in Britain were inundated by people asking for CDs and tapes of that particular song. People then went on to ask about other things which Pavarotti sang, so that the retailers found it difficult to keep up the supply. There was a further effect on the BBC. The "Third Programme" is a classical music program that tends to cater to those with highly developed tastes in that area. The people who were now turning to classical music asked for more popular presentations. At that point, the BBC "Third Programme" appointed a new director. A great deal was made of how this person needed to hold the interest and support of sophisticated listeners, while at the same time encouraging a growing number of uninformed but interested people. A radio critic, speaking about the situation, commented that it was all a matter of "providing accessible points of entry" for all concerned. That could have formed the title of a lecture to preachers.

The second story concerns the famous painting by Rembrandt called *The Nightwatch*, in the Rijks Museum in Amsterdam. In its original form it was larger than it is today. But the authorities in Amsterdam decided that it would fit nicely between two doorways in the Town Hall, and then discovered that they would have to crop it in order to make it fit. As a result, three people from the original painting are now missing from the present one! The Charles Wesley hymn, "For all my Lord was crucified, For all, for all my Savior died" should be a haunting refrain for all preachers in their preparation.

Before dealing with the text in its context, we reflect on the congregation that also has a contextual setting. One of the great strengths of the ministry of Jesus was the way in which he went to people where they were. Paul, traveling to cities he did not know, went to find people in their natural situations, both religious and secular.

A preacher these days will find congregations in their church setting, but their contexts are far wider than the church premises. Who they are and what is happening to them is an important consideration for the preacher who prepares a sermon. Since worship is a presenting of the whole of life to God, our preaching should help people to discern and celebrate the presence of God in the whole of life. Congregations will do this most effectively when they recognize that what they hear in the sermon relates directly to the context of life for them.

There is, for example, a liturgical context for each congregation. On one occasion, when preparing to lead a citywide mission, I visited a variety of churches that would be participating in the mission simply to introduce myself during the act of worship, and to say something about the mission itself. On Saturday evening I preached at a Roman Catholic mass. On Sunday morning I went first to a charismatic Anglican Church, where laypeople led most of the worship, where children ran around the church while the service proceeded, where there was clapping and dancing and a wholly dedicated attitude of relaxed worship. From there I went to a Presbyterian church, with Scottish origins. The worship was led by gowned and ordained ministers. The people in the congregation sat in dignified rows, wearing their best outfits. The service was carefully ordered, and whatever humor there was, remained at best, restrained. From there I went in the afternoon to an ecumenical gathering, with charts and overhead projectors, a musical group singing and playing modern music from Taize, Iona, and evangelical writers. In the evening I went to yet another Anglican Church, where there was a full-blown band, no great sense of liturgical shape, but a gallery packed with young university students who listened intently to a biblical exposition. I would not begin to judge which of these groups of Christian people was worshiping God more appropriately than others. It seemed to me that each was worshiping God according to the liturgical pattern that best suited them. What I did have to judge was how differently my material needed to be presented in such varied contexts. The way Paul gives his own testimony on three separate occasions in the Acts of the Apostles (20:17-35; 21:37–22:21; 26:1-19), to very different groups, is an instructive example.

The different liturgical contexts are affected by historical and geographical contexts also. The Roman Catholic Church where I spoke at mass on a Saturday evening, for example, discovered that it would have far more people on a Saturday evening than on the Sunday morning. Situated on the edge of an estate of publicly owned houses, it was reaching a culture where Sunday church going was not the practice, but where Saturday evening provided a possibility. One of the Anglican churches I visited on a Sunday was similarly placed near to what is usually referred to as a working-class population. The finer points of Anglican liturgy were not judged to appeal best to that population, but a free and easy, readily understood, experientially based act of worship would. The Presbyterian church was not only a place of worship but also a gathering ground for those with Scottish origins, many of whom had flourished in that particular city. The Anglican church I attended in the evening has grown up from almost no congregation twenty years previous, with a deep exploration of the implications of charismatic Christianity, and a strong appeal to students in their search for faith. No preacher going to any of these congregations dare ignore the historical and geographical context that is the setting for the sermon.

There is also, as this book has already shown, the context of local and world news, the public arena, which cannot be ignored. We dare neither preach from a first-century text as though nothing had happened since, nor offer people our opinions on modern affairs as though God had not revealed himself in Jesus Christ. A university preacher put the matter rather sharply:

> It remains an axiom of Christian preaching that the road from study to pulpit runs through a living, demanding interrupting manse; out into the noisy street; in and out of houses and hospitals, farms and factories, buses, trains, cinemas . . . up between rows of puzzled people to the place where you are called to preach. . . . For the living Word there is no bypass road from study to pulpit.[1]

This emphasis on context does not mean that the sermon must be peppered with references to the context, nor with points that are directly aimed at gathering up some part or other of that context. But it does mean that in the preparation, the preacher will have in her or his study the sense of the congregation present. I have heard it said of one great preacher that he prepared a least some of each of his sermons in the pulpit itself, occasionally looking up to ask himself how this or that point would be intelligible or helpful to this or that member of the congregation. It is the sense that they are "in the room" as the preparation is being done that is the important point. I still recall the force of a discovery I made when, having been a seminary teacher for years, and having gathered many erudite illustrations in the appropriate files, I became a circuit pastor, preaching at the same church Sunday after Sunday. The erudition of my illustrations seemed not to be setting anyone on fire! But the first time I said, "I don't know how many of you saw the television program the other evening . . . ," the entire congregation seemed to sit up! I was at last referring to something that was part, or could have been part, of all our experience. I was at last speaking to to their context. In a similar, though more refined vein, I remember hearing Robert Shaw, Conductor Emeritus of the Atlanta Symphony Orchestra, saying that he found it difficult to accept warmly many Victorian hymns, largely because the music seemed to show no capacity for pain. The question for the preacher about the congregation is, "Who are they, and what is happening to them?" The more we know about the answer to that question, the more it is part and parcel of our preparation, the more direct is the impact of the preaching likely to be.

Text to Context to Text

From context the preacher turns back to text. It might be felt that the task of linking a first-century text to a twentieth-century context is an impossible one. Indeed that argument has been eloquently made.[2] How can a first-century text have anything to say to a twentieth-century setting that is so different in every way?

But there are strong qualifications to that question, particularly to putting it that way. In the first place, although cultures change from age to age and place to place, there are fundamental elements of life that are common to all. There is birth and family, growth and learning, failure and success, relationship and solitude, happiness and sadness, questions and answers, illness and death. These are the issues with which the biblical material fundamentally deals. They are the issues that primarily make us people, and reflect our lives as human beings. And they are common to humanity in all times and all places.

Second, we have to remember that the biblical material has not suddenly been discovered in the late-twentieth century. It has been in the possession of the people of God throughout the twenty centuries that have elapsed. In the hands of God's people, that material has been taken from culture to culture, from place to place, through experience after experience, in a long tradition of faith. It has been pondered and prayed over, translated and preached about, expounded and applied, in every age and culture. What we receive is not straight out of the first century. It comes to us from the hands of others of a previous generation who received it from the previous generation and so on. The adaptation has taken place, but with faithfulness to the original text.

In the third place we have to remember that the Holy Spirit, who inspired the writers of the Scripture, has inspired God's people over the centuries, and will now inspire us as to the meaning of the Scripture for today. We are not left alone.

In the fourth place we must recall that Christian people have discovered more and more in the biblical material as centuries have developed, and as new challenges have come to the Christian faith from a variety of contexts. So we need not come to the exposition of the text with dread about there being no connection. Rather we may come with a sense of trust and excitement, knowing that God has still more light to cast upon this Holy Word.

As to what form that confident search will take, different preachers will find the ways that most enable them to grapple with biblical material. What follows is a suggestion that this preacher has found useful, based on the advice and guidance of other preachers and theologians over the years. It is not offered as a blueprint, but as one way against which other ways will be set.

A Suggested Method

There is nothing to replace the reading of the text in its context. If one is dealing with a verse, then to have some idea of how that verse fits into its particular chapter is of course important. If one is dealing with a longer section, then to know how that fits into the context of a particular letter or book is also helpful. But the real task is to read the passage itself, again and again and again. In that task it is helpful to keep in front of one the question, "*What does it say?*" At this point one needs to be certain that one understands what particular words are saying, especially those with heavy theological content, or with technical meaning. To be clear about the words, so that as we read again and again we find ourselves becoming familiar with them all, is the first step. A lexicon, or a commentary that deals with the meaning of particular words, can be most helpful at this point.

The second question goes beyond what is being said. It asks what the passage, or the particular verse, *actually means.* There are two essential helps to this process. One is to have help from commentaries (and each preacher will establish opinions about which commentaries and series are more helpful than others). At this point, the use of hermeneutical approaches becomes significant. The other is to try to write out in our own words what we believe the passage to be saying. It is very difficult to gloss over a word or a phrase or a sentence if one has to write it out in one's own language.

The next step, still dealing with meaning, is to list the major points that are being made, and then the supporting statements for those major points, and so on. If one finds oneself now dealing with main headings, subheadings and sub-subheadings, then that is simply an implication of the complexity of the text, and of the size of our task as preachers.

A third step is to move beyond the question of what it says and what it means to the question, *"How does it apply?"* This is really a matter of dealing with the text, seeing what it says, hearing its message, but at the same time looking around us at what is happening in our world locally, nationally, and internationally, and hearing the voices that speak so stridently or plaintively there, demanding or requesting our attention. The question now for the preacher is whether notes and tones are emerging from the text that harmonize with notes and tones from the news. Or are there points being made in the text that directly address issues in the news, or in the lives of the people to whom one is to preach? The exercise is almost like that of two trapeze artists swinging across space and reaching out for each other .

All of that is basic preliminary work. I find it good at that point to leave the work on the sermon for a while, in order to let the ideas and the questions, the possibilities and the problems, settle down in my mind. If one has the time, there is a lot to be said for giving oneself a day away from it all, though truth to tell a preacher rarely gets very far from a sermon in preparation.

On returning to the text, there will be questions that now have raised themselves, and we may need to go back to the commentaries and to the meanings of words and phrases in their context. There may be questions again about the historical setting of the passage, or about references that call up other passages. And there may be a variety of points at which the text seems to apply to modern life.

The major task now is to determine what is the main point, or which are the main points, which seem to have risen to the top in one's sense of importance for this particular sermon. The list of major and minor points will help here. So will the outline we have written in our own words. What we are now doing is seeking to identify the elements that will be major parts of the sermon in its development, and those places where we believe these points will apply to the life of our hearers, to the life of the church, and to the life of the world at local, national, and international levels. In terms of a previous chapter, we are dealing in the areas of event and interpretation, projection, and application.

If these things are reasonably clear, we now turn to the question of testimony. We are asking how the theological truths we wish to affirm, and their implication for daily living, can find illustration and testimony in the lives of ordinary people. It is at this point that the rooting of the sermon in the earth of everyday life becomes vitally important. We are seeking to communicate that what we are describing actually happens to people like those of us who are at worship, and therefore could be part of their experience too. This is for some preachers the most difficult area of their preparation and their preaching. Some find it helpful to gather files of illustrations and testimonies. What's important is to develop the art of seeing and hearing what is happening around us, in such a way that, whether we write it down or not, it becomes available to us under the pressure of theological truth and the state of modern life in the context of preaching.

These are but the bare bones in a preacher's preparation, and they are offered simply because so many preachers ask for help in this area, long after they have been introduced to complex hermeneutical issues in seminary.

Literary Forms of Scripture

We turn in the third place to the question of the breadth of materials available in the biblical texts. These provide us not only with a variety of literature to use. They also provide us with models in our concern to be interesting as well as true.

There are, for example, *stories*. In both Old and New Testaments this is a primary method of communication. Its major use by Jesus is at once both surprising and disturbing. I have often wondered how Jesus' way of speaking would have survived the sermon class that so many theological students have been through in seminary. In that exercise a student conducts an act of worship including a sermon, and then it is up to the congregation of students and staff, then or later, to offer their criticisms. I imagine Jesus telling one of his parables as his sermon. There would be comments about a lack of introduction and lack of conclusion. It would be pointed out that there were not three clear points (or more recently, that the "moves" in the sermon were not apparent). There would be questions about where the theological content was. It would even be asked whether proper application had been made. In the main, it would probably be said, what was offered was not a sermon but a children's address. So much for Jesus Christ, preacher.

But suppose the story *is* the theology. Suppose Jesus can speak about sheep and goats, about servants and masters, about children and parents, about building and about customs, because that is how his heavenly Father has built the world. Suppose these are the building blocks of which theology is constructed, which he affirmed in his incarnation. Suppose he is saying that these are the materials through which we are meant to discern the presence of God, just as death and resurrection in all our life cycles is present if we can perceive it, and is the very rhythm that he himself took up in order to redeem us. If these things are true, then the

———————121

story carries the whole theology within itself, without being self-consciously theological or academic.

The lesson for the preacher is twofold. There are many occasions when we do well simply to tell a biblical story again, preferably in a way that relates it to present day circumstances, and renders it both intelligible and attractive. At a major university, where I was lecturing to seminary students of various denominations on the subject of mission, I asked them at the end of the first day for their comments on whether what I was doing was helpful to them. One of them said something that quite took my breath away, but was supported by all the rest. "Will you tell us some more Bible stories please?" he said. These were graduate theological seminary students to whom I had told some of the Gospel stories in modern idiom.

But the second implication of the importance of story in the Gospels is the value of using stories ourselves in our sermons. The story is more than a piece of information. It is an invitation to people to identify the story, to identify their own stories, and if they wish to step into the story and be participants in it. Many who went to see the musical *Godspell* were surprised to find themselves invited onto the stage at the interval to mix with the performers. That is what a story is meant to do.

But there are also *concepts*. The Bible story is carried along by the interlinking of concepts. Creation is one. Kingdom is another. Salvation is another. They are like the centerpiece to a web, linking many incidents, statements, and experiences to themselves in such a way that they make intelligible what might otherwise be a disparate collection of words and ideas. These concepts provide the parameters for the preacher's understanding, focal points for the variety of things he or she learns in study and reflection, joining points that carry forward the whole story of God's dealing with the world. These concepts help us to know where we are on our journey, and they will help the congregations too if we are faithful in communicating them.

In the third place, in the interlinkage between the concepts, there are *words that are heavy with theological meaning*. They often provide a good deal of the content on which the major concepts rely. So you have a word like *righteousness*. Righteousness in the biblical material is often used of God. It is about God being right, doing right, and (as in the Letter to the Romans) putting people in the right. Such words require careful study and deep reflection about their meaning and application. But think of the relevance of that particular word to our prison policy today. Or to the work of the legal profession, or to the larger justice concerns at national and international level. These great theological words are like markers for our preacher's course. They should be a constant part of our proclamation. If we have moved away from needing theological markers, we may be going astray altogether as preachers.

Then, fourth, there are *images*. Reference has already been made to the images in John's Gospel, the great I AM sayings. Images are different from concepts and words full of theological content. They contain an unknown quantity. The images, by definition, are not the reality. But they invite you to engage with the reality by allowing the image, the picture, to lead you forward. It invites you to enter into its possibilities, to fly with it and see where you end up. An image is an invitation to a journey. It is not an unrestricted journey, nor one without guidelines. To use some of the Johannine pictures, for example, the image of bread *is* about bread, and light about light. These are determinants in themselves. In the Christian context they are also about Jesus as bread and Jesus as light. So the images are not an invitation to move away from Jesus, or to find oneself in areas contrary to his life and teaching, or his ministry as a whole. But they do invite us to explore the meaning of Jesus as bread and light in a way that engages with modern society, and they take us where we did not imagine we would go. They form one of the greatest challenges that the preacher has to offer.

More significantly, the image is increasing in our culture as a major mode of communication. Television, video, and computer are based on communicating through images. More and more people are learning through the use of the image, which is very different from learning by word. We are increasingly becoming an image-dominated culture, partly through the activity of the media. This does not automatically mean that we preachers must have pictures to hold up or overhead projectors to use. But at least it may well mean that we ought to be using word images much more than we are, and concepts much less than we do.

In the fifth place there are *values*. In the teaching of Jesus, for example, there is the value set upon the poor. They are not treated as being better than the rich, nor more automatically good than the rich. But because they are poor, and not having all that God intended for them, there is a peculiar value set upon them. The same is true about the inner state of a person. In a world where so much attention is paid to outward appearance and performance, Jesus draws attention to the inner world of attitude and motive as being much more significant. There is his emphasis on eternal life, rather than simply on years and hours and minutes. The New Testament is full of values that inform our lives. The preacher needs to be aware of what these values are, since the engagement with modern society requires them. In many discussions, they are what we have most to offer. They also inform our daily living, and are a vital part of our making sense of things. A preacher does well to test her or his sermon by the question of how much Christian value was present there.

In the sixth place there are *principles*. The distinction between principle and application has already been dealt with. Here it is the status of the principle with which we are concerned. If Jesus is at the heart of Creation, as John 1:1-8, Colossians 1:16, and Hebrews 1:2 suggest, then that which

God revealed in the life of Jesus Christ is more than simply good advice for happy living. The Word made flesh provides a revelation of principles by which the world is meant to operate. The fact that by giving one's life away one truly possesses it is one fundamental element. The fact that the lowly vulnerable route of loving care for others is the force that survives death is another. So is the judging of time in its relationship to eternity. There is something here that is written into the way God has made the world, which should be primary in our understanding of the world, and basic to our living in it. The world, facing so many difficult situations, needs to know what these principles are. Unless the preachers declare them, how will people know?

So, also, there are *commandments*. The modern world's fear of a God who issues instructions has influenced us too far in the other direction. The picture we need is not of a God who sits somewhere in heaven issuing separate instructions to separate people or groups of people. That medieval image is well behind us. But we cannot avoid the question of a moral universe. If God made the world to be part of a moral construction, then certain things will work properly and others will not, according to their moral quality. At a physical level we soon become conversant with this way of working. My office was on the third floor of the Westminster Central Hall in London. If at the end of the day I had been delayed, and needed to get quickly to my train, I knew that the quickest way down to the road from my third floor office was out through the window. I also knew that it would not be the wisest way to go for the train! Neither life, nor I, are constructed to operate like that. The moral universe is the same. There are certain ways of behaving that will produce health, and others that will not. The commandments that we find in the Scripture are God's signposts to the healthy way to live one's life in a moral universe. People need to hear the commandments of the Lord. They also need to know that the preachers they listen to are part of the operation of the moral universe.

In the eighth place, there are also *promises*. One of the great aspects of the biblical story from beginning to end is that God gives promises, and that God keeps promises. Whatever our circumstance, therefore, there is always room for hope. Preachers mislead congregations if they give an impression that the gospel is about life always being confident, or victorious, or happy. To follow Jesus is not to find that life is from then onward comfortable, assured, and prosperous. Some of the greatest moments of Christian witness take place when followers of Jesus find themselves in extremely untoward circumstances, where there seems to be no light at all, and yet they go on believing. They can do so because they believe God to be trustworthy, and they can hold on to the promises that God has given. Perhaps too much of our preaching contains demands on the congregation. People are often only too aware of the demands life makes upon them, and of their failures to meet those demands. Their greatest need may well be the promise that there is forgiveness for the penitent, that a new start is always possible, that God's love is greater than anything we are capable of ourselves, and that underneath are the everlasting arms. One of our greatest privileges as preachers is to assure people of the content of the promises, and of the trustworthiness of the one who makes them. We are meant to be hopeful preachers.

Images of the Preacher

It is perhaps a postscript, but nonetheless a fascinating one, as we consider the task of preaching, to note the metaphors and similes that are used in the New Testament to describe the preacher's task. Paul sees himself as a *gardener* and a *builder* (1 Cor. 3:5-15). Concerned about whether his work will stand the test, he emphasizes his role in nurturing the Christian church, and contrasts the use of wood and hay and stubble on the one side, and gold and iron on the other. The test of his building will be by fire. We may pause to ask what difference it makes to a preacher who sees her or his task like that of the gardener or builder.

Paul also likens his preaching work to that of the *artist* (Gal. 3:1). He asks the Galatians how they could possibly turn away from Christ, when he personally had portrayed Christ crucified before them, like an artist painting the scene. Those whose business is words need not have canvases, paint, and brushes. They are nevertheless challenged to paint verbal pictures, to use language in such a way that people see in their mind's eye the sketches that are being drawn, the color, the depth and the movement. The preacher is meant to be producing that which bears scrutiny from all kinds of angles, in all kinds of light, in a way that will continue to invite and enchant.

The preacher is also seen to be like a *doctor*. God's Word is meant to be a healing balm. It is meant to bind up wounds and heal diseases. It even has about it the power to amputate that which is no longer useful (Heb. 4:12-13). Since healing and holiness are from the same root, we are in the spiritual medical business. I recall a university teacher who went to hear one of the students preach, then say that it was a perfectly drafted sermon, with all the scholarship and the reading properly done. The sermon was well put together and well presented. But it never quite touched the teacher because, as he put it to me, "The tutor needed to hear that his sins were forgiven." People bring into the congregations so many wounds and cuts, so many forms of spiritual disease and need, so many ways in which they need the nutrition that will make them well. What does it mean to the preacher to be viewed as a doctor?

Then the preacher is also a *herald*. In 1 Corinthians 1:23, the apostle says that "we preach Christ crucified." Literally, "We herald Christ crucified." The herald in the Greek city state went ahead at the games, announcing the details, the places, and the ways in which people could enroll and participate. The herald was not telling about himself. He was pointing to something else. He also went ahead of the king, to announce the time that the king was coming and its significance. Although we cannot, and must not try to avoid the fact that preaching is through us as individuals, and therefore we matter; and although we cannot avoid the context and character of the people to whom we preach as significant to the preaching task, yet we must constantly remind ourselves that we are fundamentally heralds. We point neither to ourselves nor to our congregations. We point to the reality of God's being, and how that being relates to us in the world that God made. We offer up its needs and its possibilities, in the light of the gospel. People should know what the details are when the herald has been.

And we are *servants* (2 Cor. 4:5). Preaching is not a lordly task. It is not meant to be a guise for telling people what to do, or for dominating their lives by clever psychological and communication tricks. We are, as Paul put it, their servants for Christ's sake. As the disciples were privileged to carry around to the hungry crowd the bread and the fish that Jesus had broken to make available to them, so the preacher is called to serve the congregation with the broken bread of God's Word, received through the Spirit from the hands of Jesus himself.

In the end we have to recognize that preaching is not so much a science as an art. It isn't about following particular laws that will ensure particular results. It is about inner perceptions and commitments, and about outer relationships and conversations. In the end there is no blueprint for the ideal preacher. That does not mean that method does not matter. Because preaching has to do with perception, intuition, and sensitivity we should take all the more seriously the processes by which we do our work. This chapter has offered patterns by which we may measure our own methodology, and the quality of our preparation. It also offers some guidelines about presentation. We turn finally, and that is the appropriate place, to the question of what kind of persons we must be if we are to preach the Word of God.

10

Preaching and the Preacher

What Kind of Persons?

This chapter is the most difficult of all to write, and the most dangerous. It is both difficult and dangerous because of the impression it can give that preachers are of a particular kind. One only has to attend a large conference of preachers to be disabused of that opinion! If we are to have the kind of variety that has been adumbrated in this book, then we will need a variety of types of persons as preacher. The other danger is that one might give the impression that at some point a preacher is a finished article. Every preacher, however, who reflects on what he or she does in the pulpit is only too aware of how far they have to go.

At a large preaching conference where I was lecturing, we came to the question time, and a middle-aged woman came to the microphone. She explained that she had only just begun to be a preacher, and was facing one of her "trial sermons" in a few weeks' time. She had not been highly educated, nor did she have work that required a high level of articulation. She said she was growing in her perception of God and the world, but felt she always failed to communicate to the congregation anything like the depth that she felt within herself. She wanted some kind of affirmation from me, as a speaker on preaching, in the hope that that would make things better. As she spoke, I could feel the members of the seminar, which was about five hundred strong, sitting forward in their seats. Almost every one of them felt that they were still, some after many, many years as preachers, going through the same experiences that she was describing. The combination of the agony of the preparation and of the sense of not having communicated what one has felt on the one hand, with the deep sense of satisfaction and excitement of having the privilege of so communicating, is probably something that never leaves a preacher. As she walked back to her place she was applauded.

As a form of affirmation, this chapter, therefore, highlights certain characteristics and qualities that one would hope to find in a preacher, and for which one continues to search inside at a deeper level. If this book is used in a group, preachers are encouraged to add to the list. What follows is one preacher offering his hopes for his own preaching, as well as for that of others.

1. Preachers need to be *spiritual people.* By that I do not mean people who separate themselves from the life of the world, develop a rather pious stance in relation to the world, and have a different manner and vocabulary from everyone else. By spiritual I mean people who perceive that there is more to life than meets the eye; who perceive that the "more to life than meets the eye" is God; and who increasingly understand that presence of God in life through Jesus Christ as Lord and Savior. They are the people of "transcendence in the midst."

The root of such spirituality is, of course, a personal knowledge of God, through Jesus Christ, by the Holy Spirit. It is an experience of living within the family of the Trinity while walking on earth. It also means living life at a deeper and broader level than those who do not have such faith. I spoke at a conference of Roman Catholic evangelists, something I never expected I would do. In the first place I didn't expect ever to find a conference of Roman Catholic evangelists! In the second place I didn't ever expect that, should there be such a thing, they would invite me to speak to them! But they do exist and I was invited. While speaking of the spiritual depths of life, I used a rosebush as an illustration, a bush that I could see growing outside the window near to where I spoke. I said that the rose could be taken as a sign that it came from a good stock, since it was a beautiful flower. It was the sign of well-tended and good quality soil, since it plainly was receiving all the nutrition it needed. It suggested that there was a good gardener, since roses of that quality do not grow wild. At the end of the session one of the men went out and brought me a rose, gave it to me and asked me to give it to my wife as their way of saying thank you for my having been there. He had added yet another level of perception in relation to the rose. But that rose also represented, as did our being together, the extravagant generosity of God in giving us such beauty and variety and involvement with his world.

People are free to choose, in relation to the rose, at which level they cease to make their interpretation. They can stay, if they wish, with the most obvious meaning that has to do with good stock, good soil, and a good gardener. But how much they miss of life if that is all they see! By spiritual preacher I mean someone who is constantly opening the eyes of his or her hearers to deeper and higher perceptions of what is actually going on in the world roundabout us.

One of those perceptions will relate to identifying the presence of the kingdom of God in the world. It means discerning what God is doing around us today. The parables of Jesus provide us with some insight into that subject. If you take the extravagant generosity of God, delineated in the parable of the vineyard laborers who all receive the same wage after varied hours of work (Matt. 20:1-16); or the wonderful possibility of a new beginning, set out so movingly in the story of the prodigal son (Luke 15:11-24); or of the immense power to break down barriers of prejudice as revealed in the story of the good Samaritan (Luke 10:25-37); then one begins to perceive where God is in his world, and to be able to testify to that presence.

This spiritual perception is also about being able to take a longer view of events. The biblical story draws attention again and again to the way in which God slowly works out divine purposes, in generation after generation, though we at times do not see quite how things are working out. Peter says that the prophets often wanted to know more than they were allowed to know, but it was made clear to them that they were speaking out for a future generation (1 Pet. 1:10-12). By contrast the pressure of our world is to begin, carry through, and complete something in our own lifetime, otherwise we feel we have achieved nothing. The spiritual woman and man perceives that there is a different timespan with God. Against the backdrop of eternity, it will be enough to contribute whatever God requires of us and enables us to bring. Our satisfaction is not in bringing everything to completion but in knowing that we are part of the onward sweep of God's great work in God's world.

The spiritual person is also one who has increasingly deep inner reserves of God-given strength and calm. It is said that when the head of the Jesuit Order was asked what he would do if the order were brought to an end, he replied, "I would say my prayers for fifteen minutes and never think about it again." Such deep wells are linked to the eternal life of God, having so taken leave of everything that they are not destroyed by the loss of anything. I take that to be the meaning of Jesus' story about the foolish builder and the foolish king, illustrating the associated verses about putting him before everything else (Luke 14:25-33). It is not about income and expense account, and offering to God everything we now know we possess. It is about budgeting everything now and in the future and forever in one massive commitment of everything to God.

Such spirituality does not have to be self-consciously displayed by the preacher. It is either a reality in our lives or it isn't. But where it is present it cannot be hidden.

Nor does it happen automatically. The time given to Bible study and prayer are plainly basic. But probably at these points we do well to play down the fact that we are preachers. The reading of the Bible and the saying of our prayers is not primarily that we might be better preachers, nor that in such activities we may perceive the material for new sermons. It is primarily that as Christian women and men, we need to know God's Word more clearly, and be deepened in our perception of God through our prayers. It is not like studying a subject in order to get a job. It is like engaging in study in order that we might be better educated people. Our Bible study and our prayer life are not so much ways in which we gain greater control of the spiritual life: they are rather ways in which God gains greater control of us.

Spirituality results from more than Bible study and prayer. It is also about reflection and perception. It is about understanding life at an ever-deeper level, through developing sensitivity to God's presence. I recall very clearly the time we moved from black and white television to color television. It happened suddenly because the black and white television began to falter. Our two sons, who were then approaching their teens, pointed out that we were coming near to Christmas, and that Christmas without a television set would be intolerable! What is more, they observed gently, this would be a good opportunity to go to color. (After we did so the black and white television seemed to recover miraculously. I have never got to the bottom of that!) The impact was amazing. The charts were in color. The clothing people wore was so much more interesting. Certain programs, not least those related to sports, at last began to have meaning. The entire ambience of an evening watching television changed. There was much more to see, which I had been missing. Spirituality operates like adding the dimensions of color to life.

It is for this reason that our capacity to illustrate will emerge from this part of our experience. I believe we make a mistake if we seek to find our illustrations from some other part of our life, from what we might call the "secular" side or the "academic" side, or even the "worldly" side. It is out of our spiritual perception of life that the deepest illustrations will come for our preaching, because they are at best part of natural theology. They are the demonstration that the gospel is not something beamed to us from a distance, but something incarnated among us, nearer than "hands and feet."

2.   I think we preachers are called to be *earthy people,* also. By that I do not mean worldly in the profligate sense. I do mean worldly in the sense that we are committed to the world around us.

Many years ago I learned to sing a Christian chorus that included the line, "And I don't feel at home in the world anymore." I knew exactly what that meant. I had come to faith in Jesus Christ, and therefore had been released from the hold of worldly ambitions, hopes, attitudes, and relationships. The Spirit of God had set me free from their control, and I was looking and walking in an entirely different direction. In that sense that chorus held a very significant truth for me and still does. Since then, however, I have also learned that it would be biblically significant to be able to sing, "And I *do* feel at home in the world *at last.*" For one of my great problems before I became a Christian was knowing how everything held together. I enjoyed my sports. I enjoyed learning. I was happy at home. I was good at relationships. But I could not for the life of me see how they all belonged together, or what meaning attached to any of them. I looked forward to high moments of each in turn, only to discover that not even the high moments could bear the expectation that I had put on them. There was "a morning after the night before" about every aspect of life. Whatever was it all about?

Then I came to faith in Jesus Christ. It was as though a centerpiece to the jigsaw puzzle had fallen into place, and every other piece was joined to it. Work, play, home, relationships, now had a central focal point. I had values by which to measure them, aims that gave them purpose, and a sense that they were all part of God's gracious generosity in giving me life itself. It took some time for me to discover that this meant that art and drama, music and literature, economics and politics, philosophy and history were also part of God's gift to the world. I do not mean by that that they are all in themselves good, and certainly not that all the stories they tell, or all the ideas they offer are in accordance with God's purpose. But in themselves they are part of God's gift of life, and to be treated with thanksgiving.

It is in this sense that I mean that preachers should be earthy people. None of us can be an expert in all these fields. Some of us will never be expert in any of these fields. But we are all made to respond to our environment and our culture, and the preacher should be as aware of and sensitive to these various aspects of culture as she or he is humanly able to be. The reason for doing this is not simply that we should be better preachers! The reason is simply that we are human beings who, by the calling of God, find ourselves in positions where others look to us as role models of the Christian faith.

It is also peculiarly true about preachers, because the setting of our preaching is the worship of Almighty God. That worship is totally misunderstood if seen as an act separate from life. I was quite horrified many years ago to read a book written by a number of prominent lay people, expressing their gratitude to the church. To my dismay, almost every one of them said how grateful they were to the church, because they could come there to worship and forget all about the pressures of everyday life.

My understanding is that we come to church precisely bringing all the pressures of everyday life so that they may be subjected again to the overall call of God to serve God wholly in every part of that life. Our hymns say that all of life is meant to be an act of praise to God. Our prayers say that at every point we wish to be dependent on God's good grace. Our offering says that everything we have and possess belongs to God, in whatever way we are called to use it. Our listening to the Word of God is our declaration that we wish to be obedient in every part of our existence. Our being together in worship is a way of affirming all women and men in the world as part of our responsibility under God. We cannot as preachers play our proper part in such an act of worship while turning our backs on the cultural life of the world.

This is a fundamental theological point. In chapter 2 we looked at one of the great moments in John's Gospel is that occasion when Jesus is told that some Greeks have come to see him. The writer of the Gospel has been holding back the idea of Jesus' "hour" having come. On one or two occasions he says explicitly, "His hour had not yet come" (John 2:4; 7:6). In John 12, however, Jesus, on hearing that Greeks have come to see him, says that his hour has now come (John 12:23). His disciples wait expectantly to hear the manifesto of the Kingdom. They are metaphorically getting out their pencils and paper, in order to keep a record of this great occasion when they at last discovered what it was that this campaign was all about. What they got was a lesson in horticulture! "Unless a grain of wheat falls into the earth and dies, it remains just a single grain; but if it dies, it bears much fruit. Those who love their life lose it, and those who hate their life in this world will keep it for eternal life" (John 12:24-25).

Every person in that crowd knew that simple lesson in farming. After all, most of them had farms of their own. How could a high theological moment be turned into a totally ordinary gardening tip?

The answer seems to be that, as John suggests at the beginning of that chapter, it was Passover time (John 12:1). This was the beginning of the days leading to Pentecost. Since Pentecost was Harvest Festival, this was the time when every person was concerned about the crops. Jesus takes this moment of interest, and uses one of the almost ordinary facts connected with it. If you want to have a crop you have to plant seeds or bulbs. If there is to be a planting, then seeds and bulbs must go under the ground, be covered over, and be to all intents and purposes dead. They are buried. But from that burying comes the vegetable, the fruit, the flower. It is a simple and inalienable fact of life.

What Jesus seems to be saying is that death and resurrection are everywhere in God's universe. It takes place with the generations, with the stars, with the seasons. I remember admiring a beautiful autumn (fall) day in the Peak District in England. The colors of russet and various other shades of brown were shining in the sun. It was one of those moments when one wished one could be an artist. I commented on the beauty to my colleague who was driving me. His response was, "Of course you recognize, Donald, that it is the beauty of death." I had never thought of it quite like that before, but without this beautiful seasonal dying, there would be no resurrection in the spring. Death and resurrection are implanted everywhere.

What Jesus was doing, therefore, in his unique dying and rising, was not inventing something new: he was taking what God had already written into life and using it in a unique way because he was a unique person. The dying and rising, unique in itself, is part of God's normal way with the world.

What then follows is even more striking. Jesus now adds, "Whoever serves me must follow me, and where I am there will my servant be also. Whoever serves me, the Father will honor" (John 12:26). So this way of death and resurrection is not only the single way of Jesus. It is to be the way of all who follow him also. This means that if Jesus in his dying and rising was uniquely using a regular feature of the Creation, and so being at one with it; so he invites his followers equally to be at one with the created world. It is in fact not a sign of high spirituality when people cut themselves off from all that is going on in the world around them. It is a denial of true spirituality. The greatest monastic saints were those who used their solitude as the place for reflecting on the world and its events. They withdrew in order to see more clearly, not to turn their back on it. The distinction is crucial.

All of this means that preachers would do well to cultivate an attitude of curiosity toward the world. If the above theological exposition is accurate, then it means that we never quite know where God will be addressing us from the midst of the world outside the life of the church. Once we perceive this, the unity of all that God has made becomes increasingly clear. The potential harmony of every part of life can at least become a hope. The preacher becomes the minstrel who plays and sings the music of that harmony, so that those who hear may have it as a central element of their lives. In such a way the people of God can celebrate the Creation of God in the name of Jesus Christ the Son of God.

3.

Spiritual and earthy, to that I want to add _"dedicated."_ I mean more than "committed to the task." I sometimes feel that one doesn't make a preacher. One either is one or one isn't. Nor is it something that you can switch on or off at will. It isn't like some extra piece of clothing that you add to what you are wearing already. Being a preacher means that the whole texture of one's life is shot through with a particular vocation and responsibility. We may not always be thinking about preaching. Indeed we must not. But one never ceases to be a preacher, whatever one is doing. There is a sensitivity to life around one, a particular sense of being called, and an awareness that the moments of preaching are not separate in themselves, but are somehow expressions of everything that we are in every moment of our lives. It is this which makes it such a high calling.

So for the preacher, anything that is learned may be grist to the mill of preaching. And for the preacher there is a never-ending task of discovering how better to know what to say, how better to understand the truth that we wish to commend, and how better to put it over. There is a sense in which one is always a novice in the school of preaching. If we are not willing constantly to be learning about the art, perhaps we should not be practicing it at all.

In particular being a preacher involves one in being a word artist. There are many other ways of communicating Christian truth, but this one depends solely upon the use of words. Gestures are of course significant, but no amount of gesture will make up for the lack of meaningful language on the part of the preacher. It was said that a university teacher in London came weekly to hear the Lord Soper preach because, among other things, he learned at least one new English word every week! Donald Soper is a dedicated user of the right word with the right meaning for the right occasion. It is a standard to which we should all aspire.

Preachers should also be *interesting people.* One of the saddest things about preachers is that when we are portrayed on television and radio, in film and novel, it is almost invariably as being dull and boring and speaking too long. We have evidently given the impression that we see our calling as involving taking a long time to say something that matters in as dull a way as possible. Yet if the claims made in this book are true, then preaching ought to be the most exciting, the most engaging, the most fascinating activity that humans could commit themselves to. It is no less than declaring the secrets of the universe, secrets that are capable of turning life upside down, of subverting the world into what it ought to be, and of showing life in all its glory and depth. How can we be dull about that?

To set ourselves the goal of being interesting does not mean simply to please those who listen to us. Nor is it to try and be endlessly funny, or engagingly shallow. But it is to have grasped the deep things of life under God, to have allowed them to pass through our own existence so that they change who we are, and so to be interesting people, who communicate fascinating truth, in interesting ways. It is not only okay to be interesting, it is absolutely necessary.

Yet this book must end by striking another note altogether. It is of the essence that the preacher be pointing a way to somewhere else, namely to God in Jesus Christ by the Spirit. That is not simply our message: it is our testimony. "Except the Lord builds the house, they labor in vain who build it" (Ps. 127:1).

Being a preacher, and doing the preaching, is an exercise in *vulnerable dependence on God.* Unless God uses what we offer, it will not be of eternal significance. As our preparation is shot through with dependent prayer, so our presentation needs to be full of the Holy Spirit's power. Not all the character in the world, nor all the method in the world can replace that. But we may gladly accept that position of vulnerability, because that coin has another side. The other side is that God accepts responsibility for us. God risks being in our proclamation. There is no greater privilege than to know that *God* called me, that God *called* me, that God called *me.*

Notes

Chapter 1, God Is Here

1. A. M. Ramsey, *God, Christ, and the World* (London: SCM, 1969). He is a former archbishop of Canterbury.
2. David E. Jenkins, *The Contradiction of Christianity* (London: SCM, 1976), p. 5
3. Ian T. Ramsey, *Christian Empiricism* (London: Sheldon Press, 1974), p. 159. *Models for Divine Activity* (London: SCM, 1973), chap. 1.
4. Peter L. Berger, *A Rumour of Angels* (London: Pelican, 1971).
5. Richard Kendall, *Monet by Himself* (London: Macdonald Orbis, 1989), p. 9.
6. Ibid., p. 12.
7. Alister Hardy, *The Spiritual Nature of Man*, 1979.
8. Ibid., p. 1.
9. Ibid.
10. Project Proposal by David Hay, "The Biology of God What Is the Current Status of Hardy's Hypothesis?" p. 6.
11. Ibid., p. 1.
12. Maurice Wiles, *God's Action in the World* (London: SCM, 1986), p. 93. Based on the Bampton Lectures.
13. Ibid., 103.
14. David Jenkins, *God, Miracle, and the Church of England* (London: SCM, 1987).
15. Ibid., p. 92.
16. Ibid.
17. John Habgood, Archbishop of York, *Confessions of a Conservative Liberal* (London: SPCK, 1988), p. 63.
18. Ibid.

Chapter 3, Doctrine as a Rhythm for Life

1. Alister E. Mcgrath, *The Genesis of Doctrine: A Study in the Foundation of Doctrinal Criticisms* (Oxford: Blackwell, 1990), p. 2.

2. Karl Barth in a 1922 address entitled "The Need and the Promise of Christian Preaching"; quoted in John R. W. Stott, *I Believe in Preaching* (London: Hodder & Stoughton, 1982), p. 148.

3. George Carey, *The New Archbishop Speaks* (Oxford: Lion, 1991), p. 136.

4. Ralph L. Lewis and Gregg Lewis, *Inductive Preaching: Helping People Listen* (Wheaton, Ill.: Crossway Books, 1983), pp. 41-42.

5. James Doberstein, translator's note to Helmut Thielicke, *The Trouble with the Church* (Hodder & Stoughton, 1966), p. 8.

6. Lewis S. Mudge, *One Church: Catholic and Reformed* (Cambridge, UK: Lutterworth, 1963), pp. 62-63.

7. R. F. R. Gardner quoted in Eddie Askew, "A Silence and a Shout" (Leprosy Mission, 1982), p. 84.

8. John Habgood, *Confessions of a Conservative Liberal* (London: SPCK, 1988), p. 100.

9. Lesslie Newbigin, *Truth to Tell, the Gospel as Public Truth* (Grand Rapids: Eerdmans: New York: WCC, 1991), p. 11.

10. Eddie Askew, *Facing the Storm* (Leprosy Mission, 1989), p. 10.

Chapter 4, Atonement, Repentance, and Conversion

1. "The fact that a cross became the Christian symbol, and the Christians stubbornly refused, in spite of ridicule, to discard it in favor of something less offensive, can have only one explanation. It means that the centrality of the cross originated in the mind of Jesus himself. It was out of loyalty to him that his followers clung so doggedly to this sign." John Stott, *The Cross of Christ* (Leicester: IVP, 1986), p. 25. Stott suggests seven other symbols that might have been chosen instead (p. 21).

2. Ibid. See also Leon Morris, *The Apostolic Preaching of the Cross* (London: Tyndale, 1955).

3. Steven H. Travis, "The Doctrine of the Atonement: A Question and an Affirmation," *Epworth Review* (Jan. 1993); 74-79: James Denny, *The Atonement and the Modern Mind* (London: Hodder & Stoughton, 1910); Stott, *The Cross of Christ*.

4. James Denney, *The Christian Doctrine of Reconciliation* (London: James Clarke & Co., 1959). For a detailed account of the various ways in which modern writers have handled these themes, see Graham Slater, "The Doctrine of the Atonement—Some Recent Responses to Key Issues," *Epworth Review* 21, no. 1, (Jan. 1994): 85-92.

5. J. McLeod Campbell, *The Nature of the Atonement* (London: Macmillan, 1900).

6. Horace Bushnell, *Christ and His Salvation* (London: Strahan & Sampson Low).

7. R. C. Moberley, *Atonement and Personality*, 1901.

8. F. W. Dillistone, *The Christian Understanding of Atonement* (Nisbet, 1968).

9. Donald English, *The Message of Mark* (Leicester: Tyndale, 1992).

10. For a brief account of postmodernism with consideration of its implications for Christian belief and mission, see David Tomlison, *The Post-Evangelical* (London: SPCK, 1995).

11. Heinrich Schiller, *Principalities and Powers in the New Testament* (Edinburgh and London: Nelson, 1961).

12. To balance wholly perjorative views on the corporations, see Richard Harries, *Questioning Belief* (London: SPCK, 1995), especially chapter 14, "The Morality of Good Business."

13. Witness the reported statement of President John Kennedy: "We have the resources; we have the technology; all we lack is the will."

14. For pointers in this direction, see Jürgen Moltmann, *The Crucified God* (London: SCM, 1974).

15. For a New Testament affirmation of this truth, see Romans 8:28-39.

16. For an examination of these as *alternatives*, see David Horrell, "Paul's Collection: Resources for a Materialistic Theology," *Epworth Review* 22, no. 2, (1995): 74-89.

17. This is particularly so when it is put so sharply by Jesus in Luke 14:25-33.

Chapter 5, Reason and Faith

1. J. J. von Allmen, ed., *Vocabulary of the Bible* (London: Allmen, 1958), p. 107.

2. T. C. Hammond, *In Understanding, Be Men* (Downers Grove, Ill.: Intervarsity, 1951).

3. Thomas A. Smail, *Different Gospels: Christian Orthodoxy and Modern Theologies* (London: SPCK, 1993), p. 13.

4. Thomas C. Oden, *Agenda for Theology* (New York: Harper & Row, 1979), pp. 112-13.

5. D. S. Wright, *Introducing Pyschology* (New York: Penguin, 1970), pp. 5-11.

6. Paul F. Johnson, *Pastoral Ministration* (Hertfordshire: James Nisbit & Co., 1964), p. 3. For a fuller treatment of this topic see, Donald English, "Theology and Personality," *Epworth Review* (Jan. 1982): 35-40.

7. Harry Blamires, *The Christian Mind* (London: SPCK, 1936), p. 42.

8. Ibid.

Chapter 6, Uniformity and Variety

1. James D. G. Dunn, *Unity and Diversity in the New Testament: An Inquiry Into the Character of Earliest Christianity* (Valley Forge: Trinity International Press), 1990.

2. Ibid.

3. Ibid.

4. C. H. Dodd, *The Apostolic Preaching and Its Developments* (London: Hodder & Stoughton, 1994).

5. For a detailed examination of thirteen different New Testament examples of varied ways in which people came to faith, with contemporary

parallels, see Donald English, *The Meaning of the Warmed Heart* (Nashville: Discipleship Resources, 1987).

6. For a fuller exposition on this point, see Donald English, *From Wesley's Chair: Presidential Addresses* (London: Epworth Press, 1979), pp. 63-74.

Chapter 7, Gospel and Life

1. See John Habgood, *Confessions of a Conservative Liberal* (London: SPCK, 1988), especially chapter 3 on church and state.

2. For detailed arguments of this case see Lesslie Newbigin, *The Other Side of 1986* (New York: WCC, 1983); *Foolishness to the Greeks* (New York: WCC, 1986); *Truth to Tell: The Gospel as Public Truth* (New York: WCC, 1991).

3. For a reflection on this task from a Christian viewpoint, see Donald English, *Into the Twenty-First Century Methodist Church* (London: Home Mission, 1995).

4. Paul Kennedy, *Preparing for the Twenty-First Century* (New York: HarperCollins, 1993). Thomas Robert Malthus, "Essay on Population" 1798.

5. Francis Fukuyama, *The End of History and the Last Man* (New York: Penguin, 1992).

6. Steve Jones, *The Language of the Genes* (New York: HarperCollins, 1994).

7. *The United Methodist Hymnal* (Nashville: Abingdon, 1989), no. 363.

8. Colin Gunton, *The One, The Three, and the Many* (Cambridge: Cambridge University Press, 1993).

9. Charles Comfort quoted by Dr. Shirley L. Thomson in *Karsh: The Art of the Portrait* (Ottowa: National Gallery of Canada, 1989).

Chapter 8, Evangelistic Content

1. William Lutz, *Doublespeak* (New York: HarperCollins, 1990).

2. Matthew Henry, *Century Bible,* Mark's Gospel, p. 159.

3. A. M. Hunter, *Interpreting the Parables* (London: SCM, 1960), p. 47.

4. R. A. Cole, *The Gospel According to Saint Mark* (Wheaton, Ill.: Tyndale, 1961), p. 90.

5. Hendrik Kraemer, *The Communication of the Christian Faith* (Surrey: Lutterworth, 1957).

6. Hunter, 45.

7. Morna D. Hooker, *The Gospel According to Mark* (London: A & C Black, 1991), p. 137 on Mark 4:30-32.

Chapter 9, Text and Context

1. David Read, 1951 Warrack Lectures, quoted in J. R. W. Stott, *I Believe in Preaching* (London: Hodder & Stoughton, 1982), p. 191.

2. D. E. Nineham, *Saint Mark* (London: Pelican, 1969), especially the "Introduction." See also *The Church's Use of the Bible,* p. 148.